THE *weekday*
LUNCHES & BREAKFASTS
COOKBOOK

THE *weekday* LUNCHES & BREAKFASTS COOKBOOK

Easy & Delicious Home-Cooked Meals for Busy Families

Mary Younkin

Author of *The Weeknight Dinner Cookbook* and Creator of BarefeetInTheKitchen.com

PAGE STREET
PUBLISHING CO.

PAGE STREET
PUBLISHING CO.

First published in 2018 by

Page Street Publishing Co.

27 Congress Street, Suite 105

Salem, MA 01970

www.pagestreetpublishing.com

Distributed by Macmillan, sales in Canada by The Canadian Manda Group.

22 21 20 19 18   1 2 3 4 5

ISBN-13: 978-1-62414-498-1

ISBN-10: 1-62414-498-5

Library of Congress Control Number: 2017953565

Cover and book design by Page Street Publishing Co.

Photography by Mary Younkin

Printed and bound in China

For my boys

Sean, Sam, Ben, and Nate

Contents

Introduction

This cookbook is filled with recipes that can be made in very little time or ahead of time for quick meals whenever you need them. Preparing a homemade meal, whether you're cooking in the morning, midday, late at night, or on the weekend, is incredibly satisfying. With a little planning, you can have great-tasting made-from-scratch meals on the table all day long.

Cheesy Italian Sloppy Joe Sliders (page 20) are a hearty lunch favorite for kids and adults. Last Minute Chicken (page 27) takes only a few minutes to prep, and you'll have lunch on the table in no time. Are you trying to eat healthier? It's easier than you might think to have a unique and incredibly delicious salad ready to go each day for lunch. Check out How to Eat a Salad Every Day (page 104) for great tips on how to make that daily salad happen.

Looking for breakfast in just a few minutes? Try a Caprese Omelet (page 125) or Tortilla Eggs (page 117). Make a pan of Blackberry Almond Baked Oatmeal (page 135) or Christmas Breakfast Enchilada Casserole (page 152), and you'll have breakfast ready to reheat through the week.

Each of the make-ahead recipes in this book has been tested for refrigerator and freezer storage. The optimal storage options for each dish are provided in the notes for these recipes. All the make-ahead recipes will reheat nicely in the microwave, on the stove, or in the oven.

In addition to the lunch and breakfast recipes, you'll find a handful of sweet and savory snacks tucked inside this book. From Pineapple Jalapeño Salsa (page 176) to Coconut Oatmeal Trail Mix Cookies (page 163) and Perfect-Every-Time Brownies (page 180), there is sure to be a snack to satisfy every craving.

Sharing my love of food and cooking for others are two of my favorite things. My hope is that this book brings you joy in the kitchen and many happy meals shared with family and friends.

Mary Younkin

Quick and Easy Lunches

Lunches are often the hardest meal to plan, and whether you're at home or on the go, the meal in the middle of the day tends to be forgotten until hunger sends us to the kitchen or the drive-through for something quick and easy.

The recipes in this chapter are both simple and tasty and will be ready to eat in twenty minutes or less. Want something hearty with a little heat? Try the Creamy Cajun Pasta (page 24). Looking for a low-carb, high-protein lunch? Korean Turkey "Lettuce Wrap" Salad (page 23) combines the flavors of my favorite lettuce wraps with the easy prep and convenience of a salad.

The Muffuletta Wraps (page 32) and Chicken Cordon Bleu Wraps (page 55) are a kid and adult favorite that you can make ahead of time and grab on your way out the door. Last Minute Chicken (page 27) is on my menu at least once a week. You can serve it right off the stove with Better-Than-Store-Bought Ranch Dip with Vegetables (page 167), or slice it for sandwiches and salads.

SPINACH COUSCOUS SALAD WITH CHICKEN AND CRANBERRIES

<table>
<tr><td>Yield:
4 servings</td><td>Nutty pasta, crisp spinach, crunchy almonds, and sweet cranberries are tossed together in this sweet and tangy salad. While the salad is absolutely delicious when it is first made and served warm, it is even better after a rest in the refrigerator, making it perfect for lunches throughout the week. I serve this salad cold, warm, and at room temperature.</td></tr>
</table>

1 tbsp (15 ml) olive oil, divided

⅔ cup (116 g) Israeli couscous

1 cup (237 ml) water

DRESSING
¼ cup (60 ml) olive oil

3 tbsp (45 ml) white balsamic or champagne vinegar

1 tbsp (15 ml) honey

½ tsp kosher salt

¼ tsp freshly ground black pepper

2 boneless skinless chicken breasts, about 1 lb (454 g)

½ tsp kosher salt

½ tsp freshly ground black pepper

8 cups (360 g) baby spinach, roughly chopped bite-size

½ cup (60 g) dried cranberries

½ cup (46 g) sliced almonds

In a medium-size saucepan over medium-high heat, warm 1 teaspoon of olive oil. Add the couscous and cook stirring frequently until lightly browned and fragrant, about 3 to 4 minutes. Add the water and cover the pan with a lid. Reduce the heat and simmer until the water is absorbed, about 10 minutes.

While the couscous is simmering, make the dressing. In a small jar or bowl, whisk together the olive oil, balsamic vinegar, honey, salt, and pepper, and set aside.

Heat a nonstick grill pan or large skillet over medium-high heat. Slice the chicken breasts in half lengthwise to make 4 thin fillets. Sprinkle with salt and pepper. Drizzle the remaining oil into the pan and swirl to coat. Add the chicken to the pan and cook without touching for 2 minutes. Turn the pieces over and cook for an additional 2 to 3 minutes. Remove from the heat and place on a cutting board. Chop the chicken into bite-size ¾-inch (2-cm) pieces.

Place the spinach in a large mixing bowl. Add the cooked couscous, chicken, cranberries, and almonds. Pour the dressing over the salad and toss well to coat.

Cook's Notes: While Israeli couscous is my preference, any miniature pasta can be substituted for the couscous in this recipe. Simply cook it per the package directions, drain well, and add to the salad.

This recipe works well with pan-fried chicken, as written above, as well as with grilled or store-bought rotisserie chicken.

PAPRIKA POTATO SKILLET WITH KIELBASA AND CORN

Yield:
4 to 5 servings

Tender potatoes, corn, and kielbasa are seasoned generously with spices to make this simple skillet meal. The recipe comes together in about twenty minutes for quick and easy lunches, and it also reheats wonderfully. I've made this recipe many times just to have it in the refrigerator for reheating at lunchtime.

6 small red potatoes (2 to 3 inches [5 to 7.5 cm] in diameter), sliced thinly, about 4 cups (900 g)

1½ tsp (9 g) kosher salt, divided

1 tsp black pepper, divided

1 tbsp (15 ml) olive oil

1 small yellow onion, diced small, about 1 cup (160 g)

1 (14-oz [397-g]) kielbasa sausage, sliced as thinly as possible

1 tsp smoked or plain paprika

½ tsp granulated garlic or garlic powder

1 cup (165 g) frozen yellow corn

2 tbsp (30 ml) water

2 tbsp (8 g) fresh Italian parsley, chopped (optional)

Rinse the potatoes, leaving them wet; do not pat dry. Place them in a medium-size glass bowl. Sprinkle the potatoes with ½ teaspoon of salt and ½ teaspoon of pepper. Stir or toss with your hands. Microwave the potatoes for 4 minutes and then stir. Microwave for an additional 2 to 4 minutes, until they are fork tender.

While the potatoes are cooking, warm the oil in a very large skillet over medium-high heat. Add the onion and kielbasa to the skillet and sauté for 4 to 5 minutes, stirring frequently. Add the hot potatoes and sprinkle with 1 teaspoon of salt, paprika, ½ teaspoon of pepper, and garlic. Stir to combine.

Lower the heat to medium and add the corn. Add the water and scrape any browned bits off the bottom of the skillet. Cook for 5 minutes, until everything is hot. Taste and add salt if needed. Sprinkle with parsley before serving, if desired.

Cook's Note: If you prefer not to use the microwave, the potatoes can be cooked in the skillet with the sausage and onions. Simply add them at the start and allow an extra 5 to 8 minutes' cooking time. Lower the heat as needed to prevent them from burning. When they are fork tender, continue with the recipe.

LEMON PARSLEY ANGEL HAIR
WITH ASPARAGUS AND MUSHROOMS

<table>
<tr><td>Yield:
4 to 5
servings</td><td>This light lemony pasta is a quick and tasty way to get lunch on the table in not much more time than it takes to cook the pasta. The recipe will work well with most vegetables, so feel free to swap broccoli for the asparagus, or skip the mushrooms and add peppers. I love the crisp asparagus with tender mushrooms in this version. It has become my personal favorite. This pasta reheats well and will keep in the refrigerator for several days.</td></tr>
</table>

8 oz (227 g) angel hair pasta

1 tbsp (15 ml) olive oil

3 large cloves garlic, minced

8 oz (227 g) cremini or white mushrooms, thinly sliced

8 oz (227 g) fresh asparagus, trimmed and cut bite-size

½ tsp chili pepper flakes

3 tbsp (45 g) butter, divided

½ bunch fresh Italian parsley, chopped small, about ¼ cup (10 g)

½ to 1 tsp kosher salt

½ tsp freshly ground black pepper

3 tbsp (45 ml) fresh lemon juice, about 1 large lemon

½ cup (50 g) freshly shredded Pecorino Romano or Parmesan cheese

Lemon wedges for serving

Cook the pasta according to the package directions. Set aside ½ cup (120 ml) of pasta water before draining. Drain and do not rinse the pasta.

Warm the oil in a large skillet over medium-high heat. Add the garlic. Sauté for about 30 seconds until fragrant.

Add the mushrooms, asparagus, chili pepper flakes, and 2 tablespoons (30 g) of butter. Stir to coat and continue stirring and cooking for about 3 minutes, until the mushrooms soften and the asparagus is bright green and slightly tender. Add the parsley and cook for 1 minute.

Add the cooked pasta and sprinkle with ½ teaspoon of salt, pepper, and lemon juice. Toss to combine. Add a splash of the reserved pasta water, about ¼ cup (60 ml), if the pasta is dry. Add an additional splash of the reserved water only if it is needed. Taste the mixture and add more salt only if needed. Stir in 1 tablespoon (14 g) of butter, and top with cheese. Serve with lemon wedges, if desired.

CHEESY ITALIAN SLOPPY JOE SLIDERS

Yield:
6 servings

These hearty sliders come together in just a few minutes, making them perfect for a quick lunch any day of the week. The meat filling is also delicious stuffed into baked potatoes or served over pasta. Just top with cheese and dig in.

I considered calling these Vegetable Lover's Sloppy Joe Sliders because they are fully loaded with peppers and mushrooms. However, after one bite, my kids and husband voted unanimously for Cheesy Italian.

1 lb (454 g) ground beef or ground turkey

½ medium onion, chopped into ¼-inch (0.5-cm) pieces, about ½ cup (80 g)

2 cloves garlic, minced

1 large green or red bell pepper, chopped into ½-inch (1-cm) pieces, about 1½ cups (138 g)

5 to 8 oz (142 to 227 g) white or cremini mushrooms, thinly sliced (optional)

1 (15-oz [425-g]) can tomato sauce

¼ cup (60 ml) ketchup

1 tbsp (17 ml) Worcestershire sauce

1½ tsp (2 g) Italian Seasoning Mix (page 185) or store-bought

1 tsp kosher salt

½ tsp freshly ground black pepper

12 slider rolls

1½ cups (168 g) freshly shredded mozzarella

In a large skillet over medium-high heat, cook and crumble the ground beef. As the beef begins to brown, add the onion and the garlic and continue cooking for about 5 minutes. When the meat has browned, drain any grease. Add the pepper and the mushrooms, if desried, to the skillet, and cook for 3 to 4 minutes.

Add the tomato sauce, ketchup, Worcestershire sauce, Italian seasoning, salt, and pepper. Bring to a boil and then reduce to simmer for 5 to 10 minutes. Scoop the hot meat mixture onto the bottom half of the slider rolls and top with cheese. Cover with the top half of the rolls. Serve immediately.

Cook's Notes: For this recipe, you'll want to crumble the meat as finely as possible as it cooks.

The filling for these sliders freezes nicely. I often double or triple this recipe for future meals and freeze individual portions for reheating as needed.

KOREAN TURKEY "LETTUCE WRAP" SALAD

Yield:
4 servings

Savory hot ground turkey in a rich and flavorful sauce tops a bowl of crunchy lettuce and cabbage, turning the classic lettuce wrap into an easy-to-eat Asian-inspired salad. Cook up a batch of the meat and portion it out for lunches all week long. To make this recipe make-ahead friendly, prep the vegetables and portion them into zip-top bags. Add a paper towel to absorb moisture and keep things fresh. Press the air out, seal, and the greens will stay fresh for several days.

1 lb (454 g) ground turkey

½ tsp cornstarch

1½-inch (4-cm) piece of fresh ginger, minced, about 2 tbsp (29 g)

4 cloves garlic, minced

⅓ cup (84 ml) low-sodium soy sauce

3 tbsp (45 ml) honey

1 tbsp (15 ml) sesame oil

2 tsp (10 ml) gochujang hot sauce

1 cup (134 g) frozen peas (optional)

1 large head green leaf or romaine lettuce, chopped bite-size

½ small head purple or green cabbage, very thinly shredded

1 large cucumber, very thinly sliced

1 bunch green onions, thinly sliced

Sriracha hot sauce or additional soy sauce for topping (optional)

In a large skillet over medium-high heat, cook and crumble the turkey. Sprinkle with cornstarch. Add the ginger and garlic, and drain the meat if necessary.

While the meat is cooking, stir together the soy sauce, honey, sesame oil, and gochujang. Pour the sauce over the meat and cook for 2 minutes, until the meat is coated and the sauce has thickened. If you're adding peas, add them to the sauce now.

Divide the lettuce and cabbage into bowls. Scoop the hot turkey over the lettuce, and top with the cucumber and green onions. Drizzle with additional hot sauce or soy sauce, if desired.

Cook's Note: Chili paste may be substituted for the gochujang in this recipe. Ground beef or ground chicken may also be substituted for the turkey.

CREAMY CAJUN PASTA

Yield:
4 to 5
servings

Whether it's made slightly spicy or fiery hot, this pasta is a favorite with my entire family. My husband has never been a big fan of pasta, but he will happily eat a plate of this spicy pasta any time I make it. I use the full amount of the spices for my family, but if you are leery of the heat, start with the lesser amount.

This pasta reheats nicely for a make-ahead lunch. Simply portion it into containers and add about a tablespoon (15 ml) of water when you are ready to reheat.

1 tbsp (17 g) kosher salt, plus more to taste

8 oz (228 g) mini penne or other small pasta

½ to 1 lb (227 to 454 g) hot Italian sausage

1 small green bell pepper, cut into thin ½-inch (1-cm) pieces, about 1 cup (92 g)

2 large cloves garlic, minced

½ cup (120 ml) heavy cream

1 tbsp (3 g) Cajun Seasoning Mix (page 184) or store-bought

2 tbsp (8 g) fresh Italian parsley, chopped (optional)

Bring a large pot of water and 1 tablespoon (17 g) of salt to a boil. Cook the pasta, until it is tender and still a bit firm. Scoop out ½ cup (120 ml) of the pasta water and set beside the stove.

While the pasta is boiling, cook and crumble the sausage in a large skillet over medium-high heat, about 5 minutes. Move the sausage to a plate.

Add the bell pepper and garlic to the hot skillet. Cook for 2 minutes, until the peppers have softened. Transfer the peppers to the plate with the sausage.

Place the skillet back over medium-high heat. Carefully pour ¼ cup (60 ml) of the reserved pasta water into the hot skillet. Use a flat spatula to scrape up the brown bits and deglaze the pan. Add the cream and Cajun seasoning to the skillet and stir to combine. Reduce the heat to medium, and let it simmer for 1 to 2 minutes, until it thickens slightly. If the pasta hasn't finished cooking yet, move the sauce off the heat until the pasta finishes.

Drain the pasta and add it to the skillet with the sauce, stir to coat well. Add the sausage and peppers to the skillet with the pasta and stir to combine. Taste, and adjust the salt only if needed. If the pasta looks dry, add an additional splash of the reserved pasta water. Sprinkle with parsley before serving, if desired.

Cook's Note: Don't panic if you forget to save pasta water to deglaze the pan. Chicken broth or plain water will also work.

LAST MINUTE CHICKEN

Yield:
8 to 10
servings

With just a few minutes' prep, this Last Minute Chicken can be made in the oven. This flavorful chicken is my go-to protein for lunches through the week.

The chicken can be cooked either on the stove or in the oven. Directions for both cooking methods are given below. The chicken is great on its own with Better-Than-Store-Bought Ranch Dip with Vegetables (page 167). It can also be sliced thin for sandwiches or chopped bite-size for soup, salad, or pasta.

2 tsp (2 g) granulated garlic or garlic powder

1½ tsp (2 g) granulated onion or onion powder

2 tsp (5 g) paprika or smoked paprika

2 tsp (2 g) dried oregano

1½ tsp (3 g) freshly ground black pepper

1 tsp kosher salt

3 lb (1.5 kg) boneless skinless chicken thighs

2 tbsp (2 g) fresh cilantro, chopped (optional)

Combine the garlic, onion, paprika, oregano, pepper, and salt in a small bowl. Sprinkle half the spices over the chicken. Turn the chicken pieces over and sprinkle the remaining spices over them. Rub the spices into the chicken, if needed, to coat well.

GRILL PAN DIRECTIONS

Heat a nonstick grill pan over medium heat. Place half the chicken in the grill pan, making sure there is a gap between the pieces. Cook the chicken without touching it for 5 minutes. Flip the pieces over and cook for 3 to 5 minutes until they're cooked through. Repeat with the remaining chicken.

BROILING DIRECTIONS

Preheat the oven to broil.

Place an oven rack 6 inches (15 cm) from the top of the oven. Put a wire rack over a large baking tray and arrange the chicken on the wire rack. Place the chicken in the oven and broil for 6 minutes. Remove the chicken from the oven, turn each piece of chicken over, and then broil for 5 to 6 minutes.

Let the cooked chicken rest for 5 minutes before serving. Sprinkle the pieces with cilantro, if desired.

Cook's Notes: My preference and go-to cooking method for this chicken is my grill pan on the stove. When I'm in a rush, the oven method is a little faster simply because I can cook it all at once. This chicken can also be cooked in a skillet on the stove or on an outdoor grill.

This recipe can be made with chicken breasts as well. Simply watch the cooking time and adjust as needed. Chicken breasts will cook faster than thighs, depending on their thickness.

THICK AND HEARTY THREE BEAN CHILI WITH SAUSAGE

Yield:
6 servings

Chili in under fifteen minutes? I'm not going to deny that initially I doubted it could be done. However, this chili is loaded with flavor. Everyone who has tried it agrees; they never would've guessed that it hadn't simmered for hours. My kids request this chili frequently and make it for themselves at least once a week.

1 lb (454 g) hot sausage (ground beef can be substituted, see Cook's Notes)

¼ cup (11 g) Mexican Seasoning Mix (page 185) or taco seasoning

1 (15.5-oz [439-g]) can Great Northern or white kidney beans, with liquid

1 (15.5-oz [439-g]) can pinto beans, with liquid

1 (15.5-oz [439-g]) can light-red or dark-red kidney beans, with liquid

1 (14.5-oz [411-g]) can diced tomatoes with juices

1 (15-oz [425-g]) can tomato sauce

1 (4-oz [114-g]) can chopped green chiles

1 cup (165 g) frozen corn

1½ cups (138 g) chopped bell peppers, frozen or fresh

OPTIONAL TOPPINGS
Corn chips
Shredded cheese
Sour cream
Chopped green onions
Chopped fresh cilantro

In a large pot over medium-high heat, cook the sausage and sprinkle with the Mexican seasoning. Crumble the meat and cook until browned, about 4 minutes. Increase the heat to high. Add all of the beans, diced tomatoes, tomato sauce, green chiles, corn, and bell peppers. Bring to a boil. Reduce the heat to medium and simmer for 5 minutes, until everything has heated through. Serve with the toppings of your choice.

Cook's Notes: One pound (454 g) of ground beef may be substituted for the spicy sausage. Increase the Mexican Seasoning Mix by 2 tablespoons (6 g) if you are using ground beef.

Black beans may be substituted for either the Great Northern or red kidney beans in this recipe, if that is your preference.

If you prefer a spicier chili, adding additional canned green chiles or using frozen or freshly roasted green chiles will provide extra heat.

CHEATER JAPCHAE

Yield:
4 servings

Japchae has been my go-to order at every Korean restaurant for as long as I can remember. I've tried countless other dishes, but I always come back to this classic glass noodle stir-fry dish. As it so happens, leftover japchae is also one of my favorite leftovers to have in the refrigerator.

Now I make japchae at home, just so that I can lunch on it for several days. While often served with chicken, beef, or pork in restaurants, this cheater version is meatless and filled with vegetables. I've been known to stash portions of japchae in the back of the fridge and keep them for myself.

This will keep well in the fridge for up to a week. I typically reheat it, but it is also tasty cold from the fridge.

5 oz (150 g) glass noodles (see Cook's Notes)

1 tbsp (15 ml) sesame oil, divided

¼ cup (60 ml) low-sodium soy sauce

2 tbsp (25 g) sugar

1 tbsp (15 ml) light flavored olive oil

½ small yellow onion, very thinly sliced, about ⅔ cup (77 g)

2 large carrots, very thinly sliced into 1-inch (2.5-cm) matchsticks, about ¾ cup (92 g)

1 small red pepper, very thinly sliced into strips, about 1 cup (92 g)

4 cremini or baby bella mushrooms, very thinly sliced, about 1 cup (66 g)

3 cloves garlic, minced

1 cup (45 g) loosely packed baby spinach

1 green onion, very thinly sliced

Bring a large pot of water to a boil and then remove from the heat. Add the noodles and let them sit covered in the hot water for 10 minutes. Drain the noodles and use kitchen shears or a knife to roughly chop the noodles into 8 10-inch (25-cm) pieces. Place the noodles in a bowl and drizzle with 1½ teaspoons (8 ml) of sesame oil. Toss to coat.

In a small bowl, mix together the soy sauce, remaining sesame oil, and the sugar. Set that aside next to the stove. Add the olive oil to a very large skillet over high heat. Adjust the heat as necessary. If the oil begins to smoke, turn it down just slightly.

Add the onion and carrots. Cook stirring constantly until they're barely softened, about 1 minute. Add the pepper, mushrooms, and garlic all at once and cook for about 30 seconds. Add the spinach and the soy sauce mixture and toss to combine. Add the noodles and cook an additional 1 to 2 minutes, tossing constantly until the noodles are hot. Remove the skillet from the heat. Sprinkle the dish with the green onion before serving.

Cook's Notes: Glass noodles are typically made from sweet potato starch. However, they taste nothing like sweet potatoes. The noodles are flavorless and will absorb the flavors of the dish. Also called cellophane noodles, mung bean threads (made with bean starch), or Chinese vermicelli, these noodles are commonly available in the Asian section of most grocery stores.

This is a fast stir-fry method. You'll use high heat and constantly toss your ingredients with tongs or a wooden spatula. The whole cooking process will take less than 5 minutes, so everything needs to be ready to go before you turn on the heat.

MUFFULETTA WRAPS

Yield:
4 servings

Traditional muffulettas are hearty sandwiches piled high with an abundance of fillings. The muffuletta wrap takes all of those amazing flavors and rolls them into a handheld wrap that is just as flavorful and yet much lighter than the original. I like to serve these wraps with pepperoncini on the side along with Better-Than-Store-Bought Ranch Dip with Vegetables (page 167).

4 (10-inch [25-cm]) flour tortillas

8 small romaine lettuce leaves, stems removed

4 oz (113 g) deli ham, very thinly sliced

6 oz (170 g) provolone

4 oz (113 g) salami, very thinly sliced

4 oz (113 g) soft mozzarella, sliced

4 oz (113 g) capicola or prosciutto

¼ cup (34 g) thinly sliced roasted red pepper

¼ cup (31 g) sliced yellow pepper, hot or mild

¼ cup (34 g) sliced black olives

Olive oil (optional)

Red wine vinegar (optional)

Down the center of each tortilla, layer the lettuce, ham, provolone, salami, mozzarella, capicola, red pepper, yellow pepper, and olives in that order. Drizzle lightly with oil and vinegar, if desired. Roll the wrap tightly around the row of ingredients in the center of the tortilla. Wrap the filled tortillas tightly in plastic wrap to hold everything together, if they won't be eaten immediately. Refrigerate until ready to serve, up to 48 hours.

Cook's Note: If you are able to find it in a store near you, jarred muffuletta, or olive salad mix, will work nicely in these wraps. Use ¾ cup (194 g) of the salad mix as a substitute for the peppers and olives listed in the recipe.

SOUTHWEST CHICKEN FAJITAS

Yield:
3 to 4 servings

Tender chicken is sautéed with bell peppers and onions in an abundance of Southwest spices to create this quick skillet lunch. Served in tortillas, scooped over rice, or simply on its own, this is a lunch that comes together in very little time. These fajitas reheat well, making them a great make-ahead lunch for work as well.

1½ tbsp (22 ml) olive oil, divided

2 medium bell peppers, sliced into ½-inch (1-cm) strips, about 2 cups (184 g)

1 medium red or yellow onion, sliced into ¼-inch (6-mm) strips, about 1 cup (115 g)

1 lb (454 g) boneless skinless chicken thighs or breasts, sliced into very thin strips

1 tbsp (3 g) Mexican Seasoning Mix (page 185) or taco seasoning

1 tbsp (15 ml) lime juice, about 1 lime

FOR SERVING
Tortillas
Fresh cilantro
Sour cream
Lime juice
Avocado
Salsa

Heat 1 tablespoon (15 ml) of oil in a large stainless steel or cast-iron skillet over high heat. Add the peppers and the onion. Toss to coat and cook for about 5 minutes, stirring occasionally until the peppers soften slightly and begin to brown.

Place the chicken in a small mixing bowl and drizzle with the remaining oil. Sprinkle the chicken with the Mexican seasoning and add the lime juice. Toss well to coat the chicken thoroughly. Add the chicken to the skillet with the peppers and onion, and reduce the heat to medium. Toss to combine, and coat everything with the seasoning.

Continue cooking, stirring occasionally, until the chicken has cooked through, about 3 to 4 minutes. Be careful not to overcook the thin strips of chicken. Remove the chicken to a plate when it finishes cooking, so it won't dry out from the heat of the pan. Serve with tortillas and the toppings of your choice.

Cook's Notes:

Substitution for 1 tablespoon (3 g) of Mexican Seasoning Mix:

¼ tsp salt

¼ tsp pepper

½ tsp ground cumin

1 tsp chili powder

¼ tsp paprika

⅛ tsp granulated garlic or garlic powder

⅛ tsp granulated onion or onion powder

⅛ tsp dried oregano

⅛ tsp crushed red pepper flakes (optional)

⅛ tsp cayenne pepper (optional)

Any variety of bell peppers may be used for this recipe. Simply combine them for a total of about 2 cups (184 g) of pepper strips. I like to use a combination of whichever different colors I have on hand.

ITALIAN PASTA SOUP WITH BEEF AND CABBAGE

Yield:
6 servings

Bite-size pasta simmers in a rich broth filled with beef, tomatoes, and Italian spices to make this flavorful soup. It comes together in very little time, making it a great option for a quick lunch on a chilly day. This soup will keep nicely in the refrigerator for several days.

1 lb (454 g) ground beef

1 small onion, diced into ½-inch (1-cm) pieces, about 1 cup (160 g)

3 cloves garlic, minced

6 cups (1.5 L) beef stock, store-bought or homemade

4 oz (114 g) small uncooked pasta (see Cook's Notes)

1 (14.5-oz [411-g]) can diced tomatoes with juices

1½ tsp (2 g) Italian Seasoning Mix (page 185) or store-bought

½ to 1 tsp kosher salt

½ tsp freshly ground black pepper

½ to 1 tsp crushed red pepper flakes

½ small cabbage, chopped into 1-inch (2.5-cm) pieces, about 4 cups (280 g)

¼ cup (10 g) fresh Italian parsley, chopped

¼ cup (45 g) freshly grated Parmesan or Pecorino Romano cheese (optional)

Heat a large pot over medium-high heat. Add the ground beef, onion, and garlic. Crumble the meat and cook until browned, about 4 minutes. Increase the heat to high. Add the stock, cover with the lid, and bring to a boil. Add the pasta, tomatoes, Italian seasoning, ½ teaspoon of salt, black pepper and red pepper flakes. Bring to a boil and reduce the heat slightly to avoid boiling over.

When the pasta is almost tender, about 10 minutes, add the cabbage and reduce the heat to medium. Simmer for about 3 minutes until the cabbage turns bright green and wilts slightly. Taste the soup and add salt if needed. Stir in the parsley. Scoop into bowls and sprinkle with cheese, if desired.

Cook's Notes: The beef stock will determine how much salt is needed for this recipe. Taste the soup before adding any salt. I typically add about ¾ teaspoon of salt to this recipe. Beef broth may be substituted for the stock in this recipe. I recommend adding 1 tablespoon (15 ml) of beef base or bouillon to bump up the flavor when substituting broth for stock.

A full teaspoon of crushed red pepper flakes in this soup is a mild amount of heat for my family. If you are more sensitive to heat or are not a fan of it, this can be left out without any issue. I recommend starting with the smaller amount and tasting the soup before adding more.

One pound (454 g) of sausage may be substituted for the ground beef in this recipe. Chopped baby spinach may be substituted for the cabbage as well.

I typically use elbow noodles, ditalini, orecchiette, or mini penne for this recipe.

CHIPOTLE LIME SHRIMP BOWLS

<table>
<tr><td>Yield:
3 servings</td><td>Chipotle and lime with a touch of honey make this shrimp incredibly flavorful. It's great in lettuce wraps or over rice, as a topping for salad, or with vegetables for snacking. My favorite way to serve it is in these hearty rice bowls with lots of tasty additions. Feel free to mix and match with your favorite ingredients to make it your own.</td></tr>
</table>

SHRIMP INGREDIENTS

1 lb (454 g) extra-large or jumbo shrimp, approximately 24 shrimp, deveined and peeled

2 tbsp (30 ml), plus 2 tsp (10 ml) light flavored olive oil, divided

3 tbsp (45 ml) fresh lime juice, about 1 medium lime

1 to 2 chipotle peppers in adobo sauce, finely minced, about ½ to 1 tbsp (5 to 9 g)

1 tsp adobo sauce (liquid from the can of peppers)

2 cloves garlic, minced

2 tsp (10 ml) honey

½ tsp kosher salt

¾ tsp ground cumin

¼ tsp cayenne pepper

SUGGESTED BOWL INGREDIENTS

4 cups (744 g) cooked rice

1 (15.5-oz [439-g]) can black beans, drained and warmed

1 fresh tomato, diced, about ½ cup (90 g)

1 large avocado, thinly sliced

4 green onions, thinly sliced

1 tbsp (1 g) finely minced fresh cilantro

Lime wedges for serving

Place the shrimp in a zip-top bag or an airtight container. Stir together 2 tablespoons (30 ml) of oil, lime juice, chipotle peppers, adobo sauce, garlic, honey, salt, cumin, and pepper. Pour the marinade over the shrimp. Seal tightly and turn to coat. Let the shrimp rest on the counter for 15 minutes.

Heat a large stainless steel pan over medium-high heat. Add the remaining 2 teaspoons (10 ml) of oil to the pan and swirl to coat. Spread the shrimp across the pan and discard any remaining marinade. Let it cook for 2 minutes. Turn the shrimp over and cook for about 1 minute, until they're pink. Increase the heat to high for 30 seconds to 1 minute to slightly reduce any liquids. Remove from the pan when they're finished cooking.

Serve the shrimp as a main dish, on top of a salad, or assemble as bowls.

Cook's Notes: The key to making this a quick and easy lunch is to buy deveined and peeled shrimp that are ready to be cooked. The chipotle peppers in this recipe may be increased for extra heat.

Allowing the shrimp to marinate for at least 15 minutes ensures plenty of flavor. Be careful not to marinate longer than 30 minutes, as the shrimp will begin to break down.

NACHO TACO SALAD

Yield:
4 to 6
servings

Frito pie meets nachos meets the ultimate taco salad in this twist on classic tacos. The ingredients are basically the same, but the result is a whole lot of fun. All the salad fixings are piled on top of cheesy, beefy nachos. Served tossed in a bowl or layered on a plate, these nachos disappear as fast as I can make them.

For an even faster lunch, swap in 3 cups (6 portions) of the make-ahead version of Best Taco Meat (page 80) for the beef, seasoning, beans, and corn listed in this recipe.

1 lb (454 g) ground beef or ground turkey

¼ cup (11 g) Mexican Seasoning Mix (page 185) or taco seasoning

1 (15.5-oz [439-g]) can black beans, drained and rinsed

1 (14.5-oz [411-g]) can corn, drained

Salt and pepper to taste

9 oz (255 g) corn chips or tortilla chips

4 cups (483 g) shredded cheddar cheese

2 cups (260 g) shredded pepper Jack cheese

8 cups (376 g) thinly sliced and chopped romaine lettuce

2 cups (322 g) diced fresh tomatoes

1 (2.25-oz [64-g]) can sliced olives, drained

2 green onions, thinly sliced

3 to 6 tbsp (45 to 90 ml) fresh lime juice, about 1 to 2 limes

OPTIONAL TOPPINGS
Sliced avocados

Salsa

Sour cream

Hot sauce

Preheat the oven to 350°F (177°C).

In a skillet over medium-high heat, cook and crumble the ground beef, about 5 minutes. Sprinkle the meat with the Mexican seasoning as it cooks. Drain any excess grease and then add the beans and corn. Stir to combine and cook for 1 to 2 minutes to warm everything. Taste and add salt and pepper as needed.

Line a large baking tray with foil. Spread half the chips across the tray. Sprinkle lightly with 1 cup (113 g) of cheddar cheese. Spread half of the meat mixture over the cheese. Sprinkle with half of both cheeses. Layer the rest of the chips over the cheese and repeat the layers. Bake for 10 minutes, or until the cheese has melted completely.

Top with lettuce, tomatoes, olives, and green onions. Squeeze lime juice over everything. Add the additional toppings to individual servings as desired. Serve immediately.

Cook's Notes: Don't hesitate to add all the Mexican Seasoning Mix when you are cooking the meat. The key to all the flavor in this taco meat is the generous amount of spices. Fresh or frozen (thawed) corn may be substituted for the canned corn in this recipe.

This recipe can be easily halved for fewer servings. Simply use 1½ cups (473 g) of Best Taco Meat (page 80) in place of the first four ingredients in this recipe. Then proceed with half measurements for the remaining ingredients.

HOT TURKEY BAGEL SANDWICHES

Yield:
4 servings

Hot bagel sandwiches are a favorite with my family for weekend lunches or weekdays when we'll be at home. They reheat well, so I don't hesitate to make extra and grab them out of the fridge. Just 30 seconds in the toaster oven or microwave and they're ready to eat.

If spicy heat makes your taste buds sing, go for the pepper Jack cheese and a generous amount of chipotle aioli. If you like your foods a little tamer, try Monterey Jack cheese and plain mayonnaise.

CHIPOTLE AIOLI
¼ cup (60 g) mayonnaise

½ small lime, juiced, about 2 tsp (10 ml)

1 chipotle pepper in adobo sauce, minced, about 1 tbsp (9 g)

1 large clove garlic, minced

⅛ tsp kosher salt

SANDWICHES
4 plain, whole wheat, or everything bagels

¾ lb (340 g) deli smoked turkey breast, thinly sliced

½ lb (224 g) pepper Jack or Monterey Jack cheese, thinly sliced

Preheat the oven to 400°F (204°C).

In a small bowl, stir together the mayonnaise, lime juice, chipotle pepper, garlic, and salt. Split the bagels and arrange them cut side up on a large baking tray. Spread the aioli on the bagels.

Place 2 to 3 slices of turkey, depending on size, draped and folded, into a pile on one half of each roll. Place 1 to 2 slices of cheese over the turkey.

Bake for 5 to 6 minutes, until the cheese has melted. Remove from the oven and close each bagel with its other half, if desired.

Cook's Notes: Bagel Thins also work well for this recipe.

When purchasing my meat in the deli, I ask for the meat to be sliced thin, but not falling apart, slightly thicker than shaved. In my experience, this is a .5 setting. I like the cheese in this recipe to be slightly thicker than the meat, at a 1 setting.

I recommend multiplying the recipe for the chipotle aioli. I love having it on hand to wake up plain sandwiches. It will keep nicely in the refrigerator for a week or two.

ASIAN CHICKEN CHOPPED SALAD

Yield:
4 servings

Asian flavors abound in this fresh and light chopped salad. The beauty of this type of salad is that the ingredients are chopped small enough to get a little bit of everything in every forkful, giving you multiple flavors and textures in every bite. This salad is a terrific make-ahead option because it packs plenty of crunch. A word of advice: If you're making this salad ahead of time, add the dressing right before eating to help preserve the crisp texture.

1 head romaine lettuce, chopped very small, about 4 cups (188 g)

½ small head of cabbage, shaved thin, about 4 cups (280 g)

1 large cucumber, peeled and chopped into ½-inch (13-mm) pieces

1 cup (118 g) frozen and thawed edamame

1 cup (134 g) frozen and thawed green peas

1 red bell pepper, sliced into thin strips, about 1 cup (92 g)

2 large carrots, thinly sliced and slivered into matchsticks, about ¾ cup (92 g)

4 green onions, thinly sliced

¼ cup (4 g) fresh cilantro, chopped

4 cups (560 g) thinly sliced cooked chicken or chopped into ½-inch (1-cm) pieces

¼ cup (27 g) slivered or sliced almonds

½ cup (23 g) wonton crisps (optional)

½ cup (72 g) peanuts, lightly salted

DRESSING
¼ cup (60 ml) olive oil

2 tbsp (32 g) soy sauce

1½ tsp (7 ml) rice vinegar

1 tsp (5 ml) sesame oil

1 tsp (7 g) honey

1 large clove garlic, minced

¼ tsp freshly ground black pepper

In a large bowl, combine the lettuce, cabbage, cucumber, edamame, peas, bell pepper, carrots, green onions, cilantro, chicken, almonds, crispy noodles if desired, and peanuts. Toss to mix. In a small jar, combine the olive oil, soy sauce, vinegar, sesame oil, honey, garlic, and pepper and close tightly with a lid. Shake well to combine. Pour the dressing over the salad and toss well to coat.

Cook's Notes: The key to an excellent chopped salad is making the ingredients small enough to fit on a fork together. Make-ahead Sticky Asian Chicken (page 76) or store-bought rotisserie chicken works very nicely in this recipe. The Asian chicken is my first choice.

DILL PICKLE CHICKEN SALAD CROISSANTS

Yield:
5 to 6
servings

Fully loaded with crisp pickles, this is a chicken salad for the most dedicated of dill pickle lovers. The chicken salad works well in sandwiches and wraps, scooped into tomatoes or avocados, and topping a garden salad too. The chicken salad will keep well for a few days in the refrigerator.

½ cup (120 g) mayonnaise

1 tbsp (15 ml) pickle juice

½ tsp freshly ground black pepper

¼ tsp kosher salt

¾ tsp dried dill

½ tsp granulated garlic or garlic powder

3 cups (420 g) cooked chicken, chopped into ½-inch (13-mm) pieces, about ½ of a large rotisserie chicken

3 large pickles, diced into tiny ⅛- to ¼-inch (3- to 6-mm) pieces, about 1½ cups (215 g)

2 green onions, thinly sliced, about ¼ cup (25 g)

5 to 6 croissants, or the bread of your choice (optional)

Green leaf lettuce, baby spinach, arugula (optional)

In a medium-size mixing bowl, stir together the mayonnaise, pickle juice, pepper, salt, dill, and garlic. Add the chicken, pickles, and onions. Stir well until everything is combined.

Split the croissants in half. Layer greens on one half of the croissant and scoop the chicken salad over the greens. Top with the second half of the croissant. Serve immediately.

WARM MEDITERRANEAN PASTA

Yield:
4 to 5
servings

Tangy artichokes and olives, sweet tomatoes, and a squeeze of lemon add a whole lot of flavor to this simple pasta dish. A sprinkling of Parmesan and parsley finishes it off, making it a fast and flavorful lunch that comes together in a flash.

This reheats nicely for a make-ahead lunch. Simply portion the pasta into containers and add about 1 tablespoon (15 ml) of water when you are ready to reheat.

1 tbsp (17 g) plus 1 tsp kosher salt, divided

8 oz (228 g) angel hair pasta

3 tbsp (45 ml) good-quality olive oil

4 cloves garlic, minced

½ tsp freshly ground black pepper

¼ to ½ tsp crushed red pepper flakes

2 cups (298 g) grape or cherry tomatoes, halved

1 (14-oz [396-g]) can quartered artichokes, drained and roughly chopped

1 (6-oz [170-g]) can black olives, drained and sliced in half

¼ cup (60 ml) fresh lemon juice, about 1 lemon

¼ cup (25 g) freshly shaved or grated Parmesan

¼ cup (10 g) fresh Italian parsley, chopped

Bring a large pot of water and 1 tablespoon (17 g) of salt to a boil. Cook the pasta, until it is tender and still a bit firm. Reserve ½ cup (120 ml) of the pasta water before draining.

Warm the oil in a large stainless steel skillet over medium-high heat. Add the garlic, 1 teaspoon of salt, pepper, and crushed pepper flakes to the oil. Sauté for 1 minute, until fragrant. Add the tomatoes and cook, stirring frequently until they soften and release some juices into the oil, about 1 minute.

Add the pasta to the skillet and toss well to coat. Add the artichokes and the olives. Drizzle lemon juice over the pasta, continue tossing, and cook for 1 to 2 minutes, until everything is warm. Add a splash of the reserved pasta water if the pasta seems a bit dry. Taste and adjust the salt and pepper as needed. Remove from the heat and sprinkle with Parmesan and parsley. Toss to combine.

Cook's Notes: Don't skimp on the oil in this recipe. It helps create the sauce and adds flavor to the final dish. Also, trust me and don't skip the parsley. It adds a great fresh flavor to the final dish.

CHEESY GREEN CHILE CHICKEN

Yield:
4 servings

Tender chicken breasts are topped with green chile and melted cheese to make this easy lunch. The chicken is great tucked into hamburger buns, sliced thin over rice or pasta, or served as is with a salad or sliced vegetables.

This chicken reheats nicely. Store in an airtight container in the refrigerator.

2 large boneless skinless chicken breasts, about 1½ lb (680 g)

¾ tsp ground cumin

½ tsp New Mexico chili powder

¾ tsp kosher salt

½ tsp black pepper

2 tsp (10 ml) olive oil

4 oz (112 g) chopped roasted green chile

4 oz (112 g) pepper Jack or Monterey Jack cheese, sliced

2 tbsp (2 g) fresh cilantro, chopped (optional)

Slice the chicken breasts in half lengthwise, making thin cutlets. If the chicken is still more than ½ inch (13 mm) thick, lightly pound the cutlets until they are an even ½ inch (13 mm) in thickness. In a small bowl, add the cumin, chili powder, salt, and pepper, and stir to combine. Sprinkle the spices over both sides of the chicken.

Warm a large stainless steel skillet over medium-high heat, add the oil, and heat until shimmering. Add the chicken in a single layer across the skillet. Cook without touching for 90 seconds. Reduce the heat to medium. Flip the chicken over and spread the green chile in a layer on top of each chicken breast. Place the sliced cheese over the green chile.

Cover with a lid and cook for 2 to 3 minutes. The cheese should be just beginning to melt over the chicken. Remove from the heat, uncover, and test the chicken for doneness. It should be white throughout with barely a hint of pink. Sprinkle the chicken with cilantro before serving, if desired.

Cook's Notes: The kitchen timer is your friend for this recipe. To avoid drying out the thin pieces of chicken, watch your meat closely and set a timer for the recommended cooking times. If the meat is thicker than ½ inch (13 mm), it may require a few extra minutes. Watch closely to avoid drying it out by overcooking.

New Mexico chili powder is my first choice for this recipe, but any chili powder will work fine.

SPICY CAJUN CHEESESTEAK SANDWICHES

Yield:
4 servings

Tender steak piled on toasted sandwich rolls is a surprisingly easy meal that requires just a few minutes' prep time spent slicing the beef. In this twist on the classic Philly cheesesteak, it is all about the spicy steak, so we're skipping the peppers, onions, and mushrooms. As much as I love adding vegetables to most recipes, you won't miss them here. The Cajun spices provide an abundance of flavor in these simple sandwiches, and they are a meat lover's dream come true.

It only takes about two minutes to sear the steak crispy on the outside and juicy inside; this really is a lightning-fast lunch. Have the rolls and cheese ready to go before you start the steak on the stove, and you'll have lunch ready almost before you know it. I like to serve these sandwiches with Better-Than-Store-Bought Ranch Dip with Vegetables (page 167) or with a simple side of oven fries. If you're not in the mood for a sandwich, this steak is also great on a salad.

1 lb (453 g) skirt or flank steak

1½ tbsp (4 g) Cajun Seasoning Mix (page 184) or store-bought seasoning

4 French sandwich rolls

2 tsp (10 ml) light flavored olive oil or refined coconut oil, divided

1 tbsp (14 g) butter

1 cup (130 g) shredded pepper Jack cheese

Slice the steak across the grain as thinly as possible. Place the slices into a medium-size bowl. Sprinkle with the Cajun seasoning and toss to coat.

Preheat the oven to 400°F (204°C).

Arrange an oven rack 6 inches (15 cm) from the top of the oven. Open the sandwich rolls and spread them across a large baking tray.

Heat a heavy flat-bottomed stainless steel skillet over medium-high heat and add 1 teaspoon of oil. Swirl to coat the pan. Add half of the meat slices and spread across the pan. Cook for 1 minute, and then use a large spatula or tongs to flip them over. Cook for 1 minute. Occasionally, a slightly larger piece will have a side that looks like it hasn't browned; if so, flip to that side again for 20 to 30 seconds. The goal is to create a crisply browned outside and a lovely juicy center for each piece.

Use a spatula to remove the meat to a plate and then repeat with a second batch. When the meat has finished cooking, add the butter to the skillet. When the butter melts, scrape up any browned bits from the pan and drizzle the pan juices over the steak bites on the plate.

Divide the steak onto the bottom half of each roll. Sprinkle the cheese over the steak. Place the open sandwiches in the oven for 3 to 4 minutes, until the bread is toasted and the cheese melts. Keep an eye on the rolls; they will go from toasted to burned in moments.

CHICKEN CORDON BLEU WRAPS

Yield:
4 servings

All the flavors of classic chicken cordon bleu are tucked into these easy wraps. Thin slices of chicken breast, ham, and cheese are wrapped inside soft tortillas with a honey mustard dressing. My kids ask for these "sandwich" wraps every week, and I'm more than happy to make them as often as they like.

3 tbsp (45 g) mayonnaise

1 tbsp (15 g) Dijon mustard

1 tbsp (15 ml) honey

4 (10-inch [15-cm]) flour tortillas

8 small romaine lettuce leaves, stems removed

6 oz (168 g) deli-sliced oven-roasted chicken breast

6 oz (168 g) deli-sliced Swiss cheese

6 oz (168 g) deli-sliced black forest ham

Whisk together the mayonnaise, mustard, and honey. Spread half the mustard sauce over the tortillas in a thin layer. Layer the lettuce, chicken, cheese, and then ham in a row down the center of the tortillas. Drizzle the remaining sauce over the ham. Roll the wrap tightly around the row of ingredients in the center.

Wrap tightly in plastic wrap to hold everything together if you're not going to eat it immediately. Refrigerate until ready to serve, up to 48 hours.

SNACK TRAY LUNCHES

Yield:
Varies

Snack Tray Lunches have been a kid (and adult) favorite in our house since my oldest son was two years old. I had a muffin tin drying on the counter, and I impulsively filled the wells with his favorite snack foods. He had a blast dipping and snacking away for his lunch that day and Snack Tray Lunches became an instant favorite. Whether you serve your snack lunches in a muffin tin, an ice cube tray, a cute bento-style box, or on a paper plate, snack foods make a great lunch option.

At home or on the go, Snack Tray Lunches are a healthier and more affordable alternative to the store-bought grab-and-go options. These foods will pack nicely into bags for school and for work as well. Use this list of our favorite options as a jumping-off point to create your own Snack Tray Lunches. Stack up some meat and cheese with your favorite crackers. Pair some fresh vegetables with various dips. Add a handful of nuts and a few berries, and lunch is done as easy as can be.

Deli meats: turkey, ham, roast beef, chicken

Cured meats: salami, prosciutto, jerky

Nuts: cashews, almonds, walnuts, pecans, peanuts

Dried fruits: raisins, apricots, banana chips, cranberries

Fresh vegetables: carrots, cucumbers, bell peppers, grape tomatoes

Miscellaneous: cheese slices, chunks, or wedges; berries, apple slices, pickles, olives, granola, crackers, tortilla chips

Condiments: Better-Than-Store-Bought Ranch Dip with Vegetables (page 167), hummus, peanut butter, yogurt, jam, mustard, salsa

Most of these ingredients can be prepped ahead of time and stored in the refrigerator or pantry until ready to serve. The vegetables can be prepped up to a week ahead and stored in an airtight container or in individual zip-top bags for lunches on the go. Tuck a paper towel into the bags or containers with vegetables to absorb moisture and help them last longer.

Cheeses and meats can be stored in separate zip-top bags or airtight containers as well. Portion the condiments into 2-ounce (57-g) lidded containers, and they'll be ready to tuck into lunch bags.

The crackers, chips, dried fruits, and nuts can be portioned into servings and stored in airtight containers in the pantry until needed.

TACO RICE

This is a super flavorful rice skillet my boys love for a quick and easy lunch. This reheats nicely, so it's a terrific make-ahead option. I usually serve it scooped into bowls with a sprinkling of lettuce and tomato, but it's also great wrapped in tortillas for a hearty burrito.

2 tsp (10 ml) olive oil

1 small yellow onion, chopped into ½-inch (13-mm) pieces, about 1 cup (160 g)

1 large red pepper, chopped into ½-inch (13-mm) pieces, about 1½ cups (224 g)

8 oz (227 g) mushrooms, sliced (optional)

1 cup (195 g) white rice

2 cups (475 ml) beef stock

1 tbsp (3 g) Mexican Seasoning Mix (page 185) or taco seasoning

3 cups (945 g) Best Taco Meat (page 80), about ½ recipe, warmed

2 to 3 tbsp (30 to 45 ml) fresh lime juice, about 1 lime

⅓ cup (50 g) crumbled Cotija cheese

¼ cup (50 g) fresh cilantro, chopped

OPTIONAL TOPPINGS
Lettuce, finely chopped

Tomatoes, chopped

Avocados, thinly sliced

Warm the oil in a large skillet over medium-high heat. Add the onion and the pepper, and cook, stirring occasionally, for 2 minutes. Add the mushrooms, if desired. Cook, stirring occasionally, until everything has softened, about 3 minutes. Transfer the vegetables to a plate.

Add the rice, beef stock, and Mexican seasoning to the skillet. Cover with a lid, and bring to a boil. Reduce the heat and simmer until the water has been absorbed and the rice is tender, about 18 minutes. Uncover the skillet and stir to fluff the rice.

Add the taco meat and the cooked vegetables to the skillet. Add the lime juice to the mixture and stir to combine. Sprinkle with cheese, cilantro, and toppings, if desired.

CHEESY CHICKEN ENCHILADA PASTA

Yield:
6 servings

All the flavor of creamy, cheesy, spicy chicken enchiladas is here in this simple skillet meal. My kids adore Mexican food, and this is one of their favorite dishes. I like to serve this skillet with fresh vegetables or a tossed salad.

1 tbsp (17 g) kosher salt, plus more as needed

8 oz (228 g) pasta, cooked

1 tbsp (15 ml) olive oil

1 small yellow onion, chopped into ½-inch (1-cm) pieces, about 1 cup (160 g)

1 large green bell pepper, chopped into ½-inch (1-cm) pieces, about 1½ cups (224 g)

½ cup (115 g) sour cream

½ cup (120 ml) red or green chile enchilada sauce

1 (15.5-oz [439-g]) can black beans, drained and rinsed

3 cups (420 g) cooked chicken, chopped bite-size

1 (10-oz [283-g]) can diced tomatoes with green chile, drained well

2 cups (260 g) shredded Mexican cheese blend, cheddar, or pepper Jack cheese

2 to 3 tbsp (2 to 3 g) chopped fresh cilantro

Bring a large pot of water and salt to a boil. Cook the pasta until it is tender and still a bit firm. While the pasta is cooking, warm the oil in your largest skillet over medium-high heat. Add the onion and pepper to the skillet, and stir to coat. Allow them to cook for about 2 minutes.

Add the sour cream, enchilada sauce, beans, and chicken to the skillet. Stir to combine, and bring to a low simmer. Add the cooked pasta and tomatoes, stir again, and taste. Adjust the salt as desired.

Stir in 1 cup (130 g) of cheese, and sprinkle the pasta mixture with the remaining cheese. Cover with a lid, and remove from the heat to allow the cheese to melt, about 5 to 10 minutes. Sprinkle with cilantro before serving.

CORN, KIELBASA, AND TOMATO CHOWDER

Yield:
4 to 5 servings

Kielbasa sausage is paired with corn and tomatoes in this creamy potato chowder that is a kid and adult favorite in our house. This chowder is frequently requested for lunches, and lucky for all of us, it comes together in very little time.

While I would typically suggest prepping all ingredients in advance, this is a recipe with enough pause between steps to allow you to prep as you go. Start the kielbasa cooking, prep the onion, and then add it. While the onion is cooking, prep the potatoes, and then add them.

I don't recommend freezing this soup. However, it will keep nicely in the refrigerator for several days. I portion it into containers and reheat for lunches through the week.

2 tsp (10 ml) olive oil

1 (14-oz [397-g]) kielbasa sausage, sliced very thin, about ⅙ inch (4 mm)

1 small onion, diced very small, approximately ¼ inch (6 mm), about 1 cup (160 g)

4 cloves garlic, minced

4 cups (950 ml) chicken stock

2 large russet potatoes, diced into ½-inch (1-cm) pieces, about 4 cups (600 g)

2 cups (330 g) frozen corn

1 (14.5-oz [411-g]) can diced tomatoes

1 tsp dried thyme

1 to 2 tsp (5 to 10 g) kosher salt, adjust as needed

½ to 1 tsp freshly ground black pepper

1 cup (240 ml) heavy cream

¼ cup (10 g) fresh Italian parsley, chopped

Warm the oil in a large pot over medium-high heat. Add the sausage and cook, stirring occasionally until browned, about 4 minutes. Transfer the sausage to a plate. Add the onion to the oil remaining in the pan, and stir to coat. Cook for 3 to 4 minutes, stirring occasionally. When the onion is tender, add the garlic and cook for 1 minute while stirring.

Add ½ cup (120 ml) of chicken stock to the pot and scrape up all the browned bits. Add the remaining chicken stock and the potatoes and increase the heat to high. Cover with a lid and bring to a boil. Cook for 6 to 8 minutes, until the potatoes are tender enough to poke with a fork.

Add the corn, tomatoes, thyme, 1 teaspoon of salt, and ½ teaspoon of pepper. Return to a simmer and add the sausage back to the pot. Remove from the heat. Add the cream and stir to combine. Taste the soup and adjust the salt and pepper, as desired. Sprinkle with parsley before serving.

Cook's Notes: The parsley adds a lovely bit of freshness to this soup, so in this case, it really isn't optional. The soup is tasty without it, but it's even better with it.

The chicken stock will determine how much salt you need in this recipe. Taste the soup before adding the salt and adjust to taste.

BLACKBERRY, BACON, AND EGG SALAD WITH MAPLE DIJON VINAIGRETTE

This is one of my favorite salads to make when berries are in season. It works well with any berry you like, but I especially love the tartness of blackberries with the salty bacon and the sweet and tangy dressing. This salad takes a few extra minutes to pull together the first time you make it, but if you make extra eggs and bacon, you'll be set for the week. The salad ingredients are written for one serving. They can be multiplied as needed.

For this salad, I typically boil several eggs and cook a tray of bacon. Then I keep both of those in the refrigerator through the week and simply chop them as I'm ready to make the salads. The bacon will reheat nicely in the microwave in just a few seconds or you can add it cold to the salad.

SALAD INGREDIENTS
2 to 3 cups (72 to 108 g) chopped salad greens of your choice

¼ cup (29 g) very thinly sliced cucumber

2 oz (57 g) blackberries

1 radish, shaved very thinly

2 to 3 slices crisp bacon, chopped into 1-inch (2.5-cm) pieces

1 hard-boiled egg, chopped

1 to 2 tbsp (7 to 14 g) candied walnuts or pecans

1 tbsp (3 g) shredded very sharp cheddar or Parmesan cheese

VINAIGRETTE INGREDIENTS
2 tbsp (30 ml) olive oil

2 tbsp (30 ml) bacon grease

2 tbsp (29 ml) maple syrup

1 tsp Dijon mustard

1 tbsp (15 ml) fresh lemon juice

¼ tsp kosher salt

¼ tsp freshly ground black pepper

⅛ to ¼ tsp cayenne pepper

In a bowl, combine the salad greens, cucumber, blackberries, radish, bacon, egg, walnuts, and cheese. In a small jar, combine the oil, grease, syrup, mustard, lemon juice, salt, black pepper, and cayenne pepper, and shake well. Drizzle the salad with the vinaigrette. Toss well.

Cook's Notes: I use a varied combination of spring mix, romaine, green leaf, arugula, and baby spinach when I make this salad. I simply combine whichever greens I have on hand.

I use a vegetable peeler to shave the radish very thin.

The dressing will make about 4 to 6 servings and will keep in the refrigerator for up to a week. When you're ready to use the dressing, bring it to room temperature or warm on the stove or in the microwave. Shake well before serving.

SOUTHWEST CHICKEN MELT SANDWICHES

Yield:
4 servings

Tangy, slightly spicy chicken meets melting cheese in these hot open-faced sandwiches that only take a few minutes to make. This is a great lunch on the busiest of days.

½ recipe of Slow Cooker Chili Lime Chicken (page 92) or 2 cups (270 g) cooked and shredded chicken

¼ cup (60 g) mayonnaise

6 oz (170 g) pepper Jack or Monterey Jack cheese, shredded, divided

4 green onions, thinly sliced, about ¼ cup (50 g), plus more for topping

Kosher salt

Freshly ground black pepper

1 loaf hearty bread such as sourdough, wheat, or potato bread, thick-cut or unsliced

Chopped cilantro (optional)

Preheat the oven to broil.

Arrange an oven rack about 6 inches (15 cm) from the top of the oven. Combine the chicken, mayonnaise, half the cheese, and green onions. Stir to combine. Taste and add salt and pepper as needed.

Slice the bread about ¾ inch (19 mm) thick. Spread it across a large baking sheet pan. Pile the chicken mixture over each slice of bread and then sprinkle with additional cheese.

Broil the sandwiches for 2½ to 3 minutes, until the cheese melts and the edges of the bread are lightly toasted. Do not walk away from the oven. Watch closely; the sandwiches will go from perfectly melted to burned in seconds. Remove from the oven and top each sandwich with additional green onions or cilantro, if desired. Serve warm.

Cook's Note: If you're using plain shredded chicken for this recipe, you'll want to season it generously with spices and whichever combination of salsa and hot sauce makes you happiest. Taste it as you season it, and make it perfect for you.

GREEN CHILE PORK STREET TACOS

Yield:
3 to 4
servings

This is a lightning-fast lunch that comes together with the help of Slow Cooker Green Chile Pulled Pork (page 79). Soft tortillas are filled with pulled pork, red onion, and cilantro. My family goes crazy over these street tacos when I make them. I keep a package of this pork stashed in the freezer for quick lunches.

2 to 2½ cups (498 to 623 g) roughly chopped Slow Cooker Green Chile Pulled Pork (page 79)

6 to 8 (6-inch [15-cm]) soft flour or corn tortillas

2 limes

¼ red onion, sliced as thinly as possible

2 tbsp (2 g) cilantro, chopped

⅓ cup (77 g) Mexican crema (see Cook's Note)

In a large skillet over medium-high heat, warm the pork. Turn it with a large spatula or stir gently to heat throughout. While the pork is warming, lightly char the tortillas one at a time over a gas flame on the stove. Alternatively, they can be warmed in a skillet over medium-high heat or in the microwave.

When the pork is hot, squeeze the juice from one lime over it. Fill the warm tortillas with pork. Top with red onion and cilantro, and then drizzle with crema. Slice the remaining lime into wedges and serve alongside the tacos.

Cook's Note: Sour cream may be substituted for the Mexican crema. The taste is the same; however, the crema is a bit thinner and will drizzle nicely over the tacos.

IN-A-HURRY WHITE CHICKEN CHILI

Yield:
4 to 5
servings

Creamy chicken chili is possible without any dairy at all. The secret is in the beans. Pureeing half the beans before adding them to the chili makes for a creamy broth. This is a mildly spicy chili that even the youngest family members enjoy. For a spicier chili, increase the cayenne and green chile in this recipe.

Because there is no dairy in this recipe, this chili freezes beautifully. I portion it into individual containers and reheat for lunches.

1 tsp olive oil

½ small onion, chopped into ½-inch (1-cm) pieces, about ⅔ cup (77 g)

3 cloves garlic, minced

4 cups (950 ml) chicken broth, divided

2 (15.5-oz [439-g]) cans Great Northern or white kidney beans, drained

1 (4-oz [113-g]) can chopped green chiles

1 tsp ground cumin

½ tsp New Mexico chili powder

½ tsp dried oregano

¼ tsp smoked paprika

¼ tsp cayenne pepper

3 cups (420 g) chopped (¾- to 1-inch [1.9- to 2.5-cm] pieces) cooked chicken

2 tbsp (30 ml) fresh lime juice, about 2 small limes

¼ to ¾ tsp kosher salt, if needed

¼ cup (50 g) fresh cilantro, chopped small

Fresh limes, for serving (optional)

Warm the oil in a large pot over medium-high heat. Add the onion and garlic to the pot. Cook, stirring frequently, until the onion is lightly browned and the skillet is fragrant, 3 to 4 minutes.

Add 3½ cups (830 ml) of chicken broth, half the beans, and the green chiles. Increase the heat to high. Place the rest of the beans and ½ cup (120 ml) of chicken broth in the blender. Puree until smooth. Pour the blender mixture into the pot. Add the cumin, chili powder, oregano, paprika, and pepper. Stir to combine. When the soup boils, reduce the heat to a simmer.

Add the chicken and the lime juice. Taste the chili and add a small amount of salt only if needed. Simmer for 2 minutes, until heated through. Stir in cilantro and scoop into bowls. Serve with an additional squeeze of lime, if desired.

Cook's Notes: The chicken broth will determine how much salt is needed for this recipe. Taste the chili before adding any salt. When using store-bought broths, I typically add about ½ to 1 teaspoon of salt to this recipe.

For the cooked chicken in this recipe, I use Last Minute Chicken (page 27), Slow Cooker Chili Lime Chicken (page 92), or store-bought rotisserie chicken.

Make-Ahead Lunches

Do you find yourself in the drive-through lane picking up food for lunch more often than you might like? Or standing in front of the refrigerator wishing something delicious would magically appear at lunchtime? This chapter is filled with simple and delicious meals designed to be made ahead of time for lunches throughout the week.

The recipes in this chapter require on average between 20 and 35 minutes of prep and cooking time. They also provide additional servings for meals through the week. Each recipe has been tested for refrigerator storage and reheating. If a recipe is recommended for freezer storage, that is noted on the specific recipe.

Are you a fan of Mexican food? Make a skillet of Best Taco Meat (page 80) and pop it in the fridge. Warm it up later for quick tacos, salads, burritos, or nachos. Slow Cooker Green Chile Pulled Pork (page 79) is another make-ahead favorite to have on hand for Smothered Green Chile Pork Burritos (page 100) or the Crispy Green Chile Pork Skillet (page 91); those lunches will come together in just a few minutes.

Three Bean, Beef, and Bell Pepper Soup (page 96) is a favorite with the whole family, and it freezes beautifully. Tuck a few containers in the freezer and you'll have lunch made for the week. Southwest Pasta Salad (page 83) comes together in very little time and keeps nicely in the fridge for several days.

Sesame Steak Stir-Fry with Green Beans (page 95) requires little more than prep time and cooks in just minutes. Vegetable Lover's Fried Rice (page 88) is a hearty meatless lunch that even the meat eaters devour.

SOUTHWEST CHICKEN SKILLET WITH CORN AND ZUCCHINI

Yield:
4 to 6
Servings

Tender, spicy bites of chicken are tossed with fresh sautéed vegetables and plenty of Mexican spices, while a squeeze of lime keeps it fresh. Serve as written below or with rice for a heartier meal. This isn't a time-intensive recipe; however, there are about twenty minutes of prep work. I frequently cook this at night or on the weekend and reheat through the week for easy lunches.

CHICKEN INGREDIENTS
1½ lb (675 g) boneless skinless chicken thighs or breasts, cut into 2-inch (5-cm) strips

2 tsp (10 ml) light flavored olive oil, divided

2 tbsp (6 g) Mexican Seasoning Mix (page 185)

VEGETABLE INGREDIENTS
1½ lb (680 g) summer squash: Italian zucchini, Mexican gray, or yellow crookneck, sliced very thin, approximately ⅛ inch (3 mm)

1 large red bell pepper, sliced into thin matchsticks, about 1 cup (92 g)

1 (11-oz [311-g]) can corn niblets, drained, or 1 cup (165 g) frozen corn

2 cloves garlic, minced, or 1½ tsp (4 g) granulated garlic or garlic powder

1½ tsp (2 g) Mexican Seasoning Mix (page 185)

2 tbsp (30 ml) fresh lime juice, about 2 small limes

2 tbsp (2 g) fresh cilantro, chopped

2 to 3 tbsp (19 to 28 g) Cotija cheese, crumbled (optional)

Place the chicken in a medium-size bowl. Drizzle with 1 teaspoon of oil. Sprinkle with the Mexican seasoning.

Heat a large skillet over medium-high heat. Add 1 teaspoon of oil to the skillet. Add the chicken and toss to coat. Cook for 3 to 4 minutes, constantly stirring until the chicken has browned and is cooked through. Transfer the cooked chicken to a plate and tent with foil to keep warm.

Add the squash, pepper, corn, and garlic to the empty skillet. Sprinkle with the Mexican seasoning. Continue cooking over medium-high heat, stirring frequently until the squash and the pepper wilt just slightly and everything is warm, about 4 minutes.

Add the chicken back to the skillet. Add the lime juice, scrape all the browned bits off the bottom of the skillet and stir, mixing the juices over the chicken and vegetables. Remove from the heat. Sprinkle cilantro and Cotija, if desired, over the skillet.

MAKE-AHEAD DIRECTIONS
Store this in an airtight container for up to three days. Reheat on the stove, in the microwave, or covered in the oven.

STICKY ASIAN CHICKEN

Yield:
6 servings

Sweet and sticky glazed chicken is a favorite on its own, tucked into sandwiches, in the Asian Chicken Chopped Salad (page 44), or served over rice. The time required to cook this chicken is minimal; however, please note the time required to marinate the meat for optimum flavor.

1½ cups (360 ml) low-sodium soy sauce

½ cup (100 g) brown sugar

3 to 6 tbsp (49 to 98 g) chili paste

4 cloves garlic, minced

2 inches (5 cm) fresh ginger, peeled and minced, about 2 tbsp (29 g)

3 lb (1.5 kg) boneless skinless chicken breasts or thighs (see Cook's Note)

2 tsp (10 ml) light flavored olive oil (for grill pan)

2 green onions, thinly sliced (optional)

Cook's Note: If your chicken breasts are thicker than ½ inch (13 mm), slice them horizontally to create thinner pieces before marinating. Very little heat is added to this recipe with 3 tablespoons (49 g) of chili paste. I add the full 6 tablespoons (98 g) for my family, and it has just a bit of heat to balance the sweet marinade.

In a bowl, whisk together the soy sauce, brown sugar, chili paste, garlic, and ginger. Set aside ¾ cup (180 ml) of the marinade. Place the chicken in a large freezer bag or airtight container. Pour the remaining marinade over the chicken and marinate in the refrigerator for 6 to 24 hours. When you're ready to cook the chicken, remove it from the marinade and follow the directions below.

BROILING DIRECTIONS
Preheat the oven to broil.

Place a rack 6 inches (15 cm) from the top of the oven. Arrange the chicken in a single layer on a large baking sheet. Broil the chicken for 5 minutes, remove the baking sheet from the oven, and turn each piece over. Broil the chicken for 4 to 5 minutes, until the pieces begin to blacken just a tiny bit. If your pieces are thicker than ½ inch (13 mm), they may require a couple of extra minutes. The inside of the meat should no longer be pink, and the juices should run clear when you cut into it.

STOVE TOP GRILL PAN DIRECTIONS
Heat a grill pan over medium-high heat. Drizzle about 2 teaspoons (10 ml) of oil across the pan and turn to coat. Add the chicken to the pan in a single layer (you will need to cook in two batches). Cook 4 to 5 minutes, or until the underside develops grill marks. Turn each piece over with a pair of tongs and cook 4 to 5 minutes, or until they're done.

When the chicken has almost finished cooking, place the reserved marinade in a small saucepan and bring to a boil. Simmer for 2 to 3 minutes, until the sauce has thickened and is slightly reduced.

Drizzle the cooked chicken with the reduced sauce and sprinkle with green onions, if desired. Alternatively, the sauce may be served on the side for dipping.

MAKE-AHEAD DIRECTIONS
Store the chicken in an airtight container for up to 3 days. Reheat on the stove or in the microwave.

SLOW COOKER GREEN CHILE PULLED PORK

Green Chile Pulled Pork is one of our favorite meats to have on hand in the refrigerator and freezer. I drop a roast in the slow cooker to make this at least once or twice a month. When it has cooked and cooled, portion the meat into containers or zip-top bags. Use this pork to top a salad, wrap it into Smothered Green Chile Pork Burritos (page 100), or pile it onto Green Chile Pork Street Tacos (page 68).

1 medium onion, thinly sliced

4 lb (2 kg) pork roast, bone-in or boneless will work fine

2 tsp (12 g) kosher salt

1 tsp black pepper

1½ tsp (2 g) dried oregano

1 tsp ground cumin

1 tsp plain or smoked paprika

½ tsp cayenne pepper

14 oz (397 g) frozen roasted green chile, chopped (mild or hot)

Fresh cilantro, chopped (optional)

Place half of the sliced onion in the bottom of a large slow cooker. (I recommend 5 to 8 quarts [4.7 to 7.6 L].) Add the roast. Combine the salt, pepper, oregano, cumin, paprika, and cayenne in a small bowl, and then sprinkle generously over all sides of the roast. Turn the roast fat side up, if applicable, in the slow cooker, and top with the remaining onion and green chile.

Cover and cook on low for 8 hours, until tender and easily pulled apart. Remove the fat cap, if there is one, and discard. Gently shred the pork, leaving plenty of larger bite-size chunks. Allow the pork to rest in the juices in the slow cooker for at least 15 minutes, tossing with tongs occasionally as it reabsorbs the liquids. If desired, sprinkle with fresh cilantro before serving or before portioning the meat into containers.

MAKE-AHEAD DIRECTIONS
Store the pork in an airtight container for up to 3 days. Reheat on the stove, in the microwave, or covered in the oven. This can be stored in one large container or portioned into single servings and frozen until ready to eat. Thaw in the refrigerator or microwave.

Cook's Notes: You can substitute the frozen green chile with 1½ cups (186 g) of fresh, roasted green chile or 14 ounces (397 g) of canned chopped green chile.

This recipe works with a sirloin tip roast as well. You'll need to add ½ cup (120 ml) of water to the slow cooker and be sure to cook the roast until it pulls apart easily. The sirloin tip roast is significantly leaner and will be tough if it isn't cooked until tender enough to fall apart. I typically use a 2-pound (1-kg) roast, halve the other ingredients in this recipe, and cook for about 9 to 10 hours on low.

BEST TACO MEAT

Yield:
6 servings

Ground beef seasoned generously with Mexican spices is combined with black beans and corn to create a versatile taco meat that is perfect for tacos, salads, burritos, quesadillas, and nachos.

I keep a batch of this taco meat portioned into individual bags and stacked flat in my freezer. I use it for our lunches at least a couple of times a week.

1½ lb (680 g) ground beef or ground turkey

⅓ cup (14 g) Mexican Seasoning Mix (page 185) or taco seasoning

1 (15.5-oz [439-g]) can black beans, drained and rinsed

1 (15.25-oz [432-g]) can corn, drained, or 1½ cups (248 g) frozen corn

1 tbsp (1 g) chopped fresh cilantro, for topping (optional)

In a large skillet over medium-high heat, cook and crumble the ground beef. Sprinkle with the Mexican seasoning as it begins to crumble. Drain any excess grease and add the beans and corn. Stir to combine. Continue cooking for 1 to 2 minutes, just to warm everything. Top with fresh cilantro just before serving, if desired.

MAKE-AHEAD DIRECTIONS

Store the taco meat in an airtight container for up to 3 days. Reheat on the stove, in the microwave, or covered in the oven. This can be stored in one large container or portioned into ½-cup (64-g) servings and frozen until ready to use. Thaw in the refrigerator or microwave.

Cook's Notes: Don't hesitate to add the full amount of spice. The key to all the flavor in this taco meat is the generous amount of Mexican seasonings.

This recipe doubles and triples easily for extra freezer portions.

SOUTHWEST PASTA SALAD

Yield:
8 to 10 servings

Much the same way that a chopped garden salad gives you an abundance of different flavors in every bite, the ingredients in this pasta salad are chopped small enough to do the same. There's a whole lot of flavor packed into this salad. I like to make this recipe on the weekend and then eat the leftovers for lunches through the week. The salad will keep well in the refrigerator for at least 3 to 4 days.

The time required to prepare this salad will vary depending on how quickly you can chop the vegetables. If you are proficient at slicing and dicing, this recipe will come together very quickly.

6 to 8 oz (171 to 228 g) tiny pasta

1 very small red onion, diced extra small, about ⅛- to ¼-inch (3- to 6-mm) pieces, approximately ½ cup (80 g)

3 cups (447 g) grape tomatoes, halved

1 small yellow bell pepper, chopped into ½-inch (1-cm) pieces, about ¾ cup (112 g)

1 (11-oz [311-g]) can corn niblets, drained

1 (2.25-oz [64-g]) can sliced olives, drained

½ cup (8 g) fresh cilantro, minced

⅓ cup (50 g) Cotija or feta cheese, crumbled (optional)

DRESSING INGREDIENTS
½ cup (120 ml) olive oil

⅓ cup (78 ml) fresh lime juice, about 4 limes

2 large cloves garlic, minced

1 tsp kosher salt

½ tsp freshly ground black pepper

¼ tsp cayenne pepper

Cook the pasta according to the package directions. Drain and rinse well to cool. While the pasta is cooking, combine the onion, tomatoes, pepper, corn, and olives in a large mixing bowl.

In a glass measuring cup or small bowl, whisk together the oil, lime juice, garlic, salt, black pepper, and cayenne pepper. Add the cooked pasta to the bowl with the vegetables, and pour the dressing over the pasta and vegetables. Stir or toss well to thoroughly coat everything. Sprinkle cilantro over the pasta and stir again. Cover with a lid and chill in the refrigerator until ready to serve. Sprinkle with cheese just before serving, if desired.

MAKE-AHEAD DIRECTIONS
Store this in an airtight container in the refrigerator for up to 4 days.

Cook's Notes: I like to use the tiniest salad pastas possible, in addition to chopping everything as small as possible. This way you'll have a bit of pasta and multiple vegetable flavors in each bite. You can find the packages of extra small Mexican pasta in the Hispanic food section of most grocery stores. The more common ditalini pasta also works well in this recipe.

I've found that the niblets style of canned corn tends to be the crunchiest; however, plain yellow canned corn works well too. Fresh corn is also tasty in this salad, either raw or lightly sautéed and cooled.

TATER TACO CASSEROLE

Yield:
8 servings

Fluffy baked potatoes are combined with spicy taco meat, black beans, and corn in this make-ahead lunch recipe. An abundance of gooey cheese tops these potatoes, making them completely and totally irresistible.

These potatoes are fantastic right out of the oven, and they reheat perfectly for lunches all week long.

2 lb (907 g) red potatoes, chopped into ¾-inch (19-mm) pieces

2 tbsp (30 ml) olive oil

1 tbsp (3 g) Mexican Seasoning Mix (page 185) or taco seasoning

3 cups (945 g) Best Taco Meat (page 80), about ½ recipe

4 oz (113 g) Monterey Jack cheese, cut into ½-inch (1-cm) cubes

4 oz (113 g) cheddar cheese, freshly shredded

¼ cup (4 g) fresh cilantro, chopped

4 green onions, thinly sliced

Preheat the oven to 450°F (232°C).

Place the potatoes in a 9 × 13-inch (23 × 33-cm) baking dish. Drizzle with oil, and then sprinkle with the Mexican seasoning. Toss well to coat the potatoes. Bake for 30 minutes.

Remove the potatoes from the oven and stir. They should be fork tender. Add the taco meat and the cubed cheese. Stir to combine, making sure the cheese is distributed evenly throughout the dish. Top with the shredded cheese.

Reduce the oven temperature to 400°F (204°C) and bake until the cheese has melted, about 15 minutes. Sprinkle with cilantro and green onions. Let rest for 10 minutes before serving.

MAKE-AHEAD DIRECTIONS
Store this dish in an airtight container for up to 3 days. Reheat in the microwave or covered in the oven. This can be stored in one large container or portioned into individual servings for storage and reheating.

Cook's Notes: Mix together the following seasonings as a substitution for 1 tablespoon (3 g) of Mexican Seasoning Mix:

¼ tsp salt

¼ tsp pepper

½ tsp ground cumin

1 tsp chili powder

¼ tsp paprika

⅛ tsp granulated garlic or garlic powder

⅛ tsp granulated onion or onion powder

⅛ tsp dried oregano

⅛ tsp crushed red pepper flakes (optional)

⅛ tsp cayenne pepper (optional)

ASIAN CHICKEN AND BROCCOLI STIR-FRY

Yield:
4 to 5
servings

Slightly spicy and just a little bit sweet, this chicken stir-fry is a great lunch to stir together in a hurry or to make ahead and reheat through the week. My kids love it with rice, while my husband and I usually eat it on its own.

1½ tbsp (23 ml) light flavored olive oil or refined coconut oil, divided

1 medium onion, sliced into thin strips, about 1½ cups (173 g)

4 cloves garlic, minced

1½ lb (675 g) boneless skinless chicken thighs, cut into 2-inch (5-cm) pieces

1½ tsp (4 g) cornstarch

⅓ cup (80 ml) low-sodium soy sauce

2 tbsp (30 ml) honey

1 tbsp (16 g) chili paste

3 cups (213 g) bite-size broccoli florets

Cooked rice for serving (optional)

Heat a large stainless steel skillet over medium-high heat. Add ½ tablespoon (7 ml) of oil, and let it warm for a few seconds. Add the onion strips and let them cook for 2 minutes. Add the garlic and stir. Push the garlic and onion to the outside of the pan.

Pour the remaining oil in the center of the skillet. Add the chicken. Spread across the skillet and sprinkle with cornstarch. Cook without stirring for 2 minutes, until browned, and then use a sturdy metal spatula to lift and flip each piece of chicken. Cook for 1 minute.

While the chicken is cooking, stir together the soy sauce, honey, and chili paste. Add the sauce to the skillet and stir to combine.

Add the broccoli on top of the other ingredients and cover with lid. Cook for 2 minutes. The broccoli should be bright green and barely softened. Remove the lid and stir, scraping up any bits of sauce or meat from the bottom of the skillet. Simmer 1 minute to thicken the sauce, stirring frequently. Serve on its own or over rice, if desired.

MAKE-AHEAD DIRECTIONS
Store this in an airtight container for up to 3 days. Reheat in the microwave or on the stove. This can be stored in one large container or portioned into individual servings for storage and reheating.

Cook's Notes: Boneless skinless chicken breasts may be substituted for the thighs in this recipe. However, breasts will cook faster, so take care not to overcook.

If you plan to serve this with rice, start the rice before you begin cooking the chicken and broccoli. The rice can be stored along with the stir-fry in individual containers. If you're storing these together, you'll want to add 1 tablespoon (15 ml) of water to the container before reheating in the microwave. If you choose not to use a microwave, I recommend storing them separately, so that both the rice and the stir-fry will reheat nicely on the stove.

VEGETABLE LOVER'S FRIED RICE

The beauty of fried rice is in the versatility of it. It's highly adaptable, making it great for those days when you need to use up random bits of produce in the refrigerator. My kids love choosing their favorite vegetables to add to the rice when we make it.

The secret to easy and perfect-every-time fried rice is having everything ready to go when you start the recipe. Stir constantly and scrape the toasted bits off the bottom of the pan as you cook the rice. This recipe goes really fast once you turn on the stove.

2 tbsp (30 ml) light flavored olive oil or refined coconut oil, divided

4 eggs, lightly beaten

¾ tsp kosher salt, divided

½ medium onion, diced small, about ⅔ cup (77 g)

½ medium red bell pepper, chopped small, about ⅔ cup (99 g)

½ medium yellow bell pepper, chopped small, about ⅔ cup (99 g)

1 to 2 tbsp (15 to 30 ml) water, as needed

1 broccoli crown, florets trimmed very small, about 2 cups (142 g)

4 large mushrooms, thinly sliced, about 1 cup (66 g)

¼ tsp freshly ground black pepper

4 cups (744 g) cold cooked rice

¼ cup (60 ml) low-sodium soy sauce

1 tbsp (15 ml) sesame oil

½ cup (67 g) frozen peas

4 green onions, thinly sliced

Warm 2 teaspoons (10 ml) of olive oil in a large stainless steel skillet over medium-low heat. Swirl the oil to coat the surface of the pan. Pour the eggs into the pan and tilt as needed to spread the eggs across the skillet. Sprinkle with ¼ teaspoon of salt. Let the eggs cook for 2 to 3 minutes and then flip. Cook for 1 minute. Slide the eggs out of the skillet onto a cutting board and allow them to cool. Cut into ½-inch (133-mm) strips, and then cut the strips into small pieces.

Add 1 teaspoon of oil to the skillet. Add the onion and toss to coat. Cook for 2 minutes, until slightly softened. Add the bell peppers. Cook for 1 minute while stirring occasionally. If the pan is too dry, add 1 tablespoon (15 ml) or so of water. Add the broccoli. Cook for 1 minute while stirring occasionally. Add the mushrooms. Sprinkle the vegetables with ½ teaspoon salt and the black pepper. Add 2 tablespoons (30 ml) of water and increase the heat to medium-high. Continue cooking for 2 minutes, until all of the vegetables have softened. Transfer the vegetables to a plate.

Add the remaining tablespoon (15 ml) of oil to the skillet. Add the rice and stir to coat. Continue stirring and cooking for 1 to 2 minutes. Add the soy sauce and sesame oil. Stir well to distribute the sauce throughout the rice. Cook for 3 minutes, stirring and scraping the bottom of the pan frequently with a metal spatula, until the rice is heated through.

Add the peas to the rice. Stir and cook 2 minutes, until everything is hot. Remove from the heat. Add the eggs, vegetables, and green onions to the skillet. Sprinkle with pepper to taste. Stir gently to mix. Taste the rice and add salt, only if needed.

MAKE-AHEAD DIRECTIONS
Store the fried rice in an airtight container for up to 3 days. Reheat in the microwave or on the stove. If the rice is too dry, add 1 to 2 tablespoons (15 to 30 ml) of water, as needed, while reheating. This can be stored in one large container or portioned into individual servings for storage and reheating.

CRISPY GREEN CHILE PORK SKILLET

Yield:
4 to 5
servings

Juicy pork, crisp potatoes, tender peppers, and onions make this a skillet meal that I'll happily eat for breakfast, lunch, or dinner. I set aside some pork to make this skillet almost every time I make Slow Cooker Green Chile Pulled Pork (page 79).

The cheese is truly optional for this recipe. I love this recipe both ways. I typically make it without the cheese, as pictured, but it's a huge favorite both ways. If you're lucky enough to have a serving or two of this recipe stashed in the refrigerator, I recommend piling it on a warm tortilla with cheese, and eating it burrito-style.

2 small russet potatoes, chopped into ½-inch (1-cm) pieces, about 2 cups (300 g)

2 tbsp (30 ml) water

2 cups (498 g) roughly chopped Slow Cooker Green Chile Pulled Pork (page 79)

1 tbsp (15 ml) olive oil, divided

½ medium yellow onion, chopped into ½-inch (1-cm) pieces, about 1 cup (160 g)

1 large bell pepper, any color, chopped into ½-inch (1-cm) pieces, 1¼ cups (186 g)

¾ tsp kosher salt, divided

½ tsp granulated garlic or garlic powder

¼ tsp black pepper

3 to 4 oz (85 to 113 g) pepper Jack and/or Monterey Jack cheeses, freshly shredded (optional)

2 green onions, thinly sliced

2 tbsp (2 g) fresh cilantro, finely minced

Place the potatoes in a glass bowl and add the water. Heat in the microwave for 2 minutes, stir, and heat for 2 minutes. Drain the water.

While the potatoes are cooking, heat a large nonstick skillet over medium-high heat. Place the Slow Cooker Green Chile Pulled Pork into the hot pan and press down with a spatula. Cook until the bottom side of the pork is crispy and browned, about 2 minutes. Transfer to a plate and tent loosely with foil.

Add 1 teaspoon of oil to the hot skillet. Let the oil warm for a few seconds and then add the onions. Toss to coat and then spread across the pan. Let them cook for 1 to 2 minutes without touching. Add the bell peppers to the skillet with the onions. Sprinkle with ¼ teaspoon of salt. Stir and cook for 2 to 3 minutes, until the peppers have softened and the onions are lightly browned. Transfer the vegetables to the plate with the crispy pork.

Add the remaining 2 teaspoons (10 ml) of oil to the skillet. Drain any extra water from the potatoes and add them to the hot oil. Sprinkle with garlic, ½ teaspoon salt, and pepper. Stir and spread across the pan. Let them cook without touching for 2 to 3 minutes, until lightly browned. Stir and cook for an additional 2 to 3 minutes.

Add the crispy meat and the vegetables back into the skillet, and toss to combine. Remove the skillet from the heat. Sprinkle the meat and vegetables lightly with cheese, if desired, and cover with a lid. Let the steam from the skillet melt the cheese for 3 to 4 minutes. Top with green onions and cilantro before serving.

MAKE-AHEAD DIRECTIONS
Store in an airtight container for up to 3 days. Reheat in the microwave or on the stove. This can be stored in one large container or portioned into individual servings for storage and reheating.

SLOW COOKER CHILI LIME CHICKEN

Yield:
6 to 8
servings

Slow cooker recipes might not be the first thing you think of for lunch, but this one requires only about five minutes to prep the ingredients and start the chicken cooking. If you start it in the morning, you can easily have the chicken ready to eat for lunch. This is also a great option for cooking on the weekend and reheating during the week.

My whole family enjoys this chicken in Southwest Chicken Melt Sandwiches (page 67) and In-a-Hurry White Chicken Chili (page 71), but it's also delicious tucked into tacos, rolled into burritos and enchiladas, or piled on a salad for a lighter meal.

3 lb (1.5 kg) boneless skinless chicken breasts or thighs

⅓ cup (14 g) Mexican Seasoning Mix (page 185) or taco seasoning

⅓ cup (78 ml) fresh lime juice, about 4 large limes

1 small onion, sliced very thin, about 1 cup (115 g)

Place the chicken in the slow cooker. Sprinkle with the Mexican seasoning and pour lime juice over the chicken. Toss with tongs to coat well. Add the onion and cover with a lid. Cook on high for 3 to 4 hours, until the chicken is tender and pulls apart with tongs or a fork.

When the chicken is easily pulled apart, shred it gently, leaving plenty of larger bites. Toss the chicken in the juices in the slow cooker. Turn off the slow cooker and let the chicken rest in the juices for several minutes to an hour. The chicken will reabsorb most of those juices.

MAKE-AHEAD DIRECTIONS
Store this in an airtight container for up to 3 days. Reheat in the microwave or on the stove. This can be stored in one large container or portioned into individual servings and frozen until ready to use. Thaw in the refrigerator or microwave.

Cook's Notes: If you are using 4 to 5 small pieces of chicken, they will cook significantly faster than 2 extra large chicken breasts. I recommend checking for doneness at about two hours if you're using especially small pieces of chicken. This chicken can also be cooked on low in the slow cooker for approximately double the recommended cooking time.

This recipe doubles and triples quite well. The shredded chicken will keep nicely in the refrigerator for several days or in the freezer for up to a month. If you plan to freeze the chicken, place it in a freeze-safe zip-top bag and remove as much air as possible prior to freezing.

If you're using store-bought taco seasoning, taste the chicken and adjust the salt and pepper as needed at the end of the cooking time.

SESAME STEAK STIR-FRY WITH GREEN BEANS

Yield:
4 servings

Tender strips of steak are marinated with soy sauce, honey, and sesame oil to make this easy lunch. I usually serve this stir-fry on its own, but it's tasty served over rice for a heartier meal as well.

Marinate the meat about half an hour before you want to eat, and you'll need less than 10 minutes to cook everything when you're ready.

1 lb (454 g) flank or skirt steak, very thinly sliced

3 cloves garlic, minced

3 tbsp (45 ml) low-sodium soy sauce, divided

2 tsp (10 ml) honey

2 tsp (10 ml) sesame oil

½ tsp crushed red pepper flakes or 2 tsp (10 g) chili paste

1 tbsp (17 g) kosher salt

1 lb (454 g) green beans, trimmed

2 tsp (10 ml) light flavored olive oil or refined coconut oil, divided

1½-inch (4-cm) section of fresh ginger, cut into very thin matchsticks, about 2 tbsp (29 g)

1 tsp sesame seeds

Place the steak, garlic, 2 tablespoons (30 ml) of soy sauce, honey, sesame oil, and pepper flakes in a medium-size bowl. Stir well to coat. Let the meat marinate on the counter for 20 to 30 minutes.

While the meat is marinating, bring a large pot of water to a boil on high heat. Add salt to the pot and then add the green beans. Cover with a lid, set a timer for 2 minutes, and bring to a boil again. While the beans are on the stove, fill a large mixing bowl with ice water. Set the bowl of ice water next to the sink and place a strainer in the sink.

When the timer beeps, check the beans. They should be almost tender but still crisp. Pour the beans from the boiling water into the strainer and then transfer them to the ice water. When the beans are cold, pour them back through the strainer and then lightly pat them dry with a tea towel.

In a very large skillet, warm 1 teaspoon of olive oil over medium-high heat. Add half the steak and spread across the skillet. Let it cook without touching it for 1 minute. Then stir or flip the pieces over frequently just until browned, about 3 minutes' total cooking time. Remove the cooked steak and any juices to a plate or bowl. Return the skillet to the heat and repeat with the remaining teaspoon of oil and the rest of the meat. Remove the cooked steak from the skillet and add it to the plate with the rest of the steak. Leave any remaining juices in the pan.

Add the last tablespoon (15 ml) of soy sauce, the green beans, and ginger to the juices left in the skillet, and sauté, tossing constantly until the green beans are hot and have absorbed the liquids.

Return the beef and any juices from the plate to the skillet. Toss quickly to combine and cook for just 1 minute to heat throughout. Remove from the heat and sprinkle with sesame seeds. Serve immediately.

MAKE-AHEAD DIRECTIONS
Store this in an airtight container in the refrigerator for up to 3 days. Reheat in the microwave or on the stove. This can be stored in one large container or portioned into individual servings for storage and reheating.

THREE BEAN, BEEF, AND BELL PEPPER SOUP

Yield: 6 to 8 servings	Chunks of beef and bell pepper fill this hearty, flavorful soup. The soup comes together in under twenty minutes and it freezes wonderfully. I like to keep containers of this soup in the freezer for lunches. This soup is a favorite with my oldest son and my husband.

2 tsp (10 ml) olive oil

1 lb (454 g) ground beef

1 tbsp (3 g) Italian Seasoning Mix (page 185) or store-bought

1 tsp kosher salt

½ tsp freshly ground black pepper

½ tsp crushed red pepper flakes (optional)

1 large onion, chopped into ½-inch (1-cm) pieces, about 1½ cups (240 g)

4 medium bell peppers, any combination of colors, chopped into ½-inch (1-cm) pieces, about 4 cups (596 g)

32 oz (946 ml) beef broth

1 (15.5-oz [439-g]) can Great Northern or white kidney beans, drained and rinsed

1 (15.5-oz [439-g]) can black beans, drained and rinsed

1 (15.5-oz [439-g]) can light-red or dark-red kidney beans, drained and rinsed

1 (15-oz [425-g]) can tomato sauce

1 (14.5-oz [411-g]) can diced tomatoes with juices

3 tbsp (45 ml) Worcestershire sauce

1 to 2 cups (130 to 260 g) freshly shredded Monterey Jack or pepper Jack cheese, for topping (optional)

Warm the oil in a large pot over medium-high heat. Add the ground beef and crumble it as it cooks. Sprinkle the meat with the Italian seasoning, salt, black pepper, and red pepper flakes as it cooks. When the meat has cooked for about 3 minutes, add the onion and bell peppers. Stir to combine, and cook for 5 minutes, until the peppers are slightly tender.

Increase the heat to high. Add the broth, the Great Northern beans, black beans, red kidney beans, tomato sauce, diced tomatoes, and Worcestershire. Stir the pot and cover with a lid. Bring to a boil, uncover, and reduce the heat, and simmer for 5 minutes. Taste the soup and adjust the salt and other seasonings as desired. Scoop into bowls and top with cheese, if desired.

MAKE-AHEAD DIRECTIONS

Store this in an airtight container in the refrigerator for up to 3 days. Reheat in the microwave or on the stove. This can be stored in one large container or portioned into individual servings and frozen for up to 2 months, until ready to use. Thaw in the refrigerator or microwave.

Cook's Note: This soup is also good with ground turkey or Italian sausage. I like it best when the peppers retain a bit of crunch; taste the soup and determine how soft you like them to be. We like the added depth that the crushed red pepper flakes give this soup; however, if you aren't a fan of any kind of heat, feel free to skip it. The soup works with and without it.

STICKY PINEAPPLE CHICKEN AND PEPPER STIR-FRY

<table>
<tr><td>Yield:
4 to 5
servings</td><td>Chicken, pineapple, and peppers are combined in a sweet and slightly spicy sauce to create this easy lunch. This simple stir-fry can be made in about twenty minutes, so it falls in the quick and easy category. However, it also reheats very well, making it a great lunch to prepare ahead of time and portion into containers for easy reheating.</td></tr>
</table>

SAUCE INGREDIENTS

1 (20-oz [567-g]) can pineapple chunks, juice only (chunks reserved)

6 cloves garlic, minced

2 tbsp (16 g) cornstarch

1 tbsp (15 ml) low-sodium soy sauce

1 tsp sesame oil

3 tbsp (38 g) light brown sugar

1 to 3 tbsp (16 to 49 g) chili paste, to taste

STIR-FRY INGREDIENTS

1 tbsp (15 ml) light flavored olive oil or refined coconut oil

1½ lb (675 g) boneless skinless chicken thighs or breasts, cut into bite-size pieces

½ tsp kosher salt

1 medium red bell pepper, sliced into ¼-inch (6-mm) strips, about 1 cup (92 g)

1 medium orange bell pepper, sliced into ¼-inch (6-mm) strips, about 1 cup (92 g)

2 green onions, thinly sliced

Cooked white rice, for serving (optional)

Whisk together the pineapple juice, garlic, cornstarch, soy sauce, sesame oil, brown sugar, and chili paste, and set the sauce next to the stove.

Heat the olive oil in a large stainless steel skillet over medium-high heat. Add the chicken and sprinkle with salt. Spread the chicken across the skillet. Let it cook for 2 minutes, until it's white and lightly browned on one side. Flip the chicken over and cook for 1 to 2 minutes, until almost cooked through. Add the red and orange bell peppers, stir, and cook for 2 minutes stirring frequently, until slightly softened and partially browned.

Pour the sauce into the skillet and stir to combine. Increase the heat as needed to bring to a simmer. Cook, stirring constantly for 2 minutes, until thickened. Add the pineapple chunks, continue stirring, and cook 5 to 6 minutes, until the sauce is sticky and everything is well coated. Sprinkle with green onions and serve over rice, if desired.

MAKE-AHEAD DIRECTIONS

Store this in an airtight container in the refrigerator for up to 3 days. Reheat in the microwave or on the stove. This can be stored in one large container or portioned into individual servings for storage and reheating.

Cook's Notes: If your can of pineapple chunks does not yield at least ¾ cup (177 ml) of juice, store-bought pineapple juice or orange juice may be added to the canned juice to reach ¾ cup (177 ml).

If you plan to serve this with rice, start the rice before you begin cooking the chicken. The rice can be stored along with the stir-fry in individual containers. If you're storing these together, you'll want to add a tablespoon (15 ml) of water to the container before reheating in the microwave. If you choose not to use a microwave, I recommend storing them separately so both the rice and the stir-fry will reheat nicely on the stove.

SMOTHERED GREEN CHILE PORK BURRITOS

Yield: 4 to 6 servings	The beauty of this recipe is in the simplicity of it. There is so much flavor in the Slow Cooker Green Chile Pulled Pork (page 79), there are no other seasonings required. You'll want to keep that pork on hand for quick and easy lunches. These burritos are a big hit with my boys every time I make them.

½ recipe Slow Cooker Green Chile Pulled Pork (page 79), cooked and shredded, about 3 to 4 cups (747 to 996 g)

4 cups (520 g) shredded cheddar, Monterey Jack, or pepper Jack cheese, divided

6 (10-inch [25-cm]) flour tortillas

1 cup (240 ml) green chile enchilada sauce

Fresh cilantro, chopped (optional)

Preheat the oven to 350°F (177°C).

Place the pork in a medium-size mixing bowl. Add half the cheese and stir or toss to combine. Scoop the meat and cheese mixture into a row in the center of each tortilla. Roll the tortilla around the meat, leaving the ends open. Place the rolled burritos, seam side down, in a 10-inch (25-cm) baking dish. Tuck the burritos into the dish tightly, side by side.

Pour the enchilada sauce over the burritos and cover with the remaining cheese. Bake for 10 to 15 minutes, until the cheese has melted. Sprinkle with cilantro before serving, if desired.

MAKE-AHEAD DIRECTIONS
These burritos can be rolled and covered with sauce and cheese ahead of time. Cover with a lid or with foil. They will keep nicely in the refrigerator that way for up to 24 hours. Add about 10 minutes to the cooking time if you're baking them cold from the refrigerator. The cooked burritos will also keep nicely in the refrigerator in an airtight container for up to 3 days. They can be reheated individually in the microwave or covered in the oven.

Cook's Notes: I use the pork cold, straight from the refrigerator.

Any combination of cheeses will work for this recipe. While my preference for this recipe is freshly shredded cheese, most of the time when I'm making these burritos, I don't take the time to shred the cheese myself. I simply use a store-bought Mexican cheese blend that I keep on hand. It works fine, and for a quick lunch, it's my go-to choice.

LUMPIA SKILLET

Yield:
4 to 5
servings

All the flavor of Filipino lumpia comes together in this one-skillet meal. Lumpia is traditionally an eggroll-style recipe with a tasty filling tucked inside a paper-thin wrapper, then fried to cook everything through. This recipe combines all of our favorite lumpia ingredients into a simple skillet meal. Served as is straight out of the pan, wrapped in lettuce, or over rice, this version of lumpia is a huge favorite. This reheats beautifully, making it a great option for a make-ahead lunch.

1 tbsp (15 ml) refined coconut oil or light flavored olive oil

1 lb (454 g) ground pork

1 tsp kosher salt, divided, plus more to taste

½ tsp freshly ground black pepper, divided

½ medium yellow onion, finely minced, about ⅔ cup (80 g)

2-inch (5-cm) section ginger, minced, about 2 tbsp (29 g)

8 cloves garlic, minced

1 (8-oz [227-g]) can sliced water chestnuts, drained, patted dry, and roughly chopped

4 to 5 large mushrooms, thinly sliced, about 1 cup (66 g)

½ head green or napa cabbage, shaved as thinly as possible, about 8 cups (560 g)

½ cup (25 g) very thinly sliced green onions

½ tsp sugar

⅓ cup (80 ml) low-sodium soy sauce

8 oz (227 g) fully cooked frozen salad shrimp, thawed and patted dry

½ cup (72 g) crushed or chopped roasted peanuts

¼ to ½ cup (60 to 120 ml) sweet chili sauce, for topping

In a large skillet over medium-high heat, warm the oil. Add the pork, crumbling it as it cooks, about 5 minutes. Sprinkle with ½ teaspoon of salt and ¼ teaspoon of pepper. Add the onion, ginger, garlic, water chestnuts, and mushrooms to the skillet. Cook and stir until the vegetables have softened and the skillet is fragrant, about 2 to 4 minutes.

Add the cabbage and green onions. Cook and toss to wilt, about 2 minutes. Add the remaining ½ teaspoon of salt, ¼ teaspoon of pepper, sugar, soy sauce, shrimp, and peanuts. Stir to combine. Cook about 2 minutes, until the shrimp is warm. Taste and adjust the salt as needed. Scoop into bowls and drizzle with sweet chili sauce before serving.

MAKE-AHEAD DIRECTIONS

Store this in an airtight container in the refrigerator for up to 3 days. Reheat it in the microwave or on the stove. This can be stored in one large container or portioned into individual servings for storage and reheating.

Cook's Note: You can find salad shrimp in the frozen section of most grocery stores. It is sold fully cooked, deveined and peeled. Simply thaw the shrimp in a strainer under cold running water. It should take only a few minutes to thaw. Canned shrimp may be substituted for the frozen and thawed shrimp in this recipe.

HOW TO EAT A SALAD EVERY DAY

Yield:
Varies

The key to making a salad happen every day is to prep all the greens and the vegetables for the salads about once a week. I usually do this on Sunday. It takes about 30 to 45 minutes, but in the end, I have salads ready to go all week without having to fuss with it each day. Store the vegetables in the refrigerator, then add protein and the toppings of your choice when you're ready to eat.

VEGETABLE OPTIONS

Chopped greens: romaine, spring mix, spinach, arugula, or butter lettuce

Tomatoes, sliced or chopped

Cucumber, sliced or chopped

Corn: canned, frozen, or fresh

Bell peppers, thinly sliced or chopped

Red onions, thinly sliced

Green onions, thinly sliced

PROTEIN OPTIONS

Best Taco Meat (page 80)

Slow Cooker Green Chile Pulled Pork (page 79)

Last Minute Chicken (page 27)

Sticky Asian Chicken (page 76)

Hard-boiled eggs

Beans

Tuna fish

Bacon

TOPPING OPTIONS

Cheese: shredded, diced, or crumbled

Avocado: sliced or diced

Fruits: diced apples or pears, orange slices, fresh berries, grapes

Plenty of crunch: croutons, tortilla chips, Fritos, nuts

Fresh lime juice or dressing of your choice

MAKE-AHEAD DIRECTIONS

Prep the vegetables and place in serving-size containers. Add a paper towel to each box to absorb moisture and help the produce last longer. Place in the refrigerator until ready to eat.

Warm the protein of your choice and chop into bite-size pieces if needed. Add the protein to the premade salad greens and vegetables. Add the toppings of your choice. Squeeze a lime generously over the salad, and sprinkle with salt and pepper. Or toss with your favorite salad dressing.

Topping Combinations

Pulled pork, avocado, Cotija cheese, lime, salt, pepper

Chicken, hard-boiled egg, cheddar cheese, ranch dressing

Chicken, berries, feta cheese, almonds or walnuts, poppyseed dressing

Tuna fish, strawberries, avocado, lime, salt, pepper

Chicken or bacon, red grapes, shaved Parmesan cheese, candied walnuts, white balsamic dressing

Taco meat, beans, corn, avocado, shredded Mexican cheese blend, lime, salt, pepper

Quick and Easy Breakfasts

We've been told for years that breakfast is the most important meal of the day, and yet our lives are so full and so busy, many of us grab something only as an afterthought when hunger pangs hit or a headache threatens.

These simple breakfasts come together in very little time. If you have just five minutes to spend in the kitchen, you can toss a batch of Slow Cooker Raisin Nut Oatmeal (page 122) in your slow cooker when you wake, and you'll have a hot breakfast waiting when you're ready to eat.

Tortilla Eggs (page 117) are a fun twist on the classic egg-in-a-hole that we ate growing up. Kids and adults love them. If you have about ten minutes, you can whip up a Caprese Omelet (page 125) that will keep you full until lunch. Cheesy Egg French Bread Breakfast Pizza (page 118) comes together in under twenty minutes and will feed a hungry crowd.

If you need a breakfast to grab on the go, Maple Cinnamon Granola Parfaits (page 110) or Chipotle Egg Salad Breakfast Sandwiches (page 113) are both terrific options.

CHEESY ITALIAN EGGS IN PURGATORY

Yield:
4 servings

My boys have all been fans of "eggs in sauce" ever since they started eating solid foods. Maybe it's the fun of dipping bread in the sauce and breaking into that perfectly soft egg, or maybe they simply love all the flavors, but I'm thrilled that they love this meal as much as the adults love it.

Traditionally, Eggs in Purgatory is made in the oven by cracking the eggs on top of the warm red sauce and then cooking them in the oven. By turning this into a stove top recipe with two skillets, it not only comes together faster, but the eggs are certain to be cooked exactly to your liking every time as well. This recipe may look like a lot of steps, but it will come together in under twenty minutes.

This sauce doubles nicely and will keep in the refrigerator for up to a week. I often pour the cold sauce into a bowl, top with cheese, and warm in the microwave for about a minute while my egg is cooking. The sauce is also excellent over pasta for a fast lunch option.

1 loaf crusty bread, for dipping

2 tbsp (30 ml) olive oil

6 cloves garlic, minced

½ tsp kosher salt

¼ tsp crushed red pepper flakes

½ tsp dried oregano

½ tsp dried basil

1 (28-oz [794-g]) can crushed tomatoes

1 tbsp (14 g) butter, divided

4 eggs

Salt and pepper

1 tbsp (15 ml) water

2 oz (56 g) freshly shredded mozzarella cheese

1 oz (29 g) shredded Parmesan cheese

1 tbsp (4 g) fresh Italian parsley, chopped small (optional)

Preheat the oven to broil. Slice the bread and spread the slices across a large baking sheet.

Warm the oil in a medium-size skillet over medium heat. Add the garlic, salt, red pepper, oregano, and basil. Shake the pan over the heat periodically or stir with a spoon. Sauté until fragrant, about 2 minutes. Add the tomatoes and simmer for 2 minutes.

While the sauce is simmering, melt ½ tablespoon (7 g) of butter in a large nonstick skillet over medium-low heat. When the butter begins to foam, tilt the pan to coat the bottom with butter. Add 2 eggs to the skillet. When the edges of the eggs turn white, season lightly with salt and pepper. Add water to the pan and cover with a lid. Cook for 2 minutes, until the eggs are done to your liking. Slide the cooked eggs onto a plate and tent with foil. Drain any liquid in the pan and add ½ tablespoon (7 g) of butter to the hot skillet. Repeat the steps with 1 to 2 more eggs.

Place the bread in the oven to toast, about 2 minutes. Watch closely and don't let it burn.

Scoop the sauce into bowls and top with mozzarella and Parmesan cheese. Sprinkle each bowl with parsley, if desired, and slide an egg over the top. Serve with crusty bread for dipping.

Cook's Note: Soft fresh mozzarella will work fine for this recipe. Simply tear or chop it into small pieces.

MAPLE CINNAMON GRANOLA PARFAITS

<table>
<tr><td>Yield:
4 servings</td><td>Sweet and crunchy granola, tangy yogurt, and fresh fruit combine in this breakfast that everyone loves. Whether you're making this for a lazy morning at home or grabbing it on your way out the door, this is a great breakfast for any day of the week.

Anytime we have granola in the house, my youngest son requests these parfaits for breakfast. I frequently make these for a late-night snack or a simple dessert too.</td></tr>
</table>

2 cups (400 g) plain Greek or traditional yogurt

½ tsp ground cinnamon

¼ tsp vanilla extract

2 tsp (10 ml) maple syrup

1 cup (122 g) Slow Cooker Nutty Coconut Granola (page 155) or your favorite store-bought granola

2 bananas, thinly sliced

1½ cups (249 g) sliced strawberries, or the berries of your choice

In a small mixing bowl, combine the yogurt, cinnamon, vanilla extract, and maple syrup. Layer the yogurt, granola, bananas, and berries into glasses, bowls, or jars. Serve immediately or cover tightly and refrigerate overnight.

Cook's Note: If you are making these parfaits ahead of time, I recommend stirring the bananas into the yogurt to prevent browning in the refrigerator.

CHIPOTLE EGG SALAD BREAKFAST SANDWICHES

Yield:
3 to 4 servings

Smoky, slightly spicy, with just a tiny bit of tang from the lime, this is an egg salad that will leave you wishing for more. I like to make up a batch of this salad and then use it for breakfasts and lunches through the week. It will keep nicely in the refrigerator for several days; just stir it up and pile it on crackers, bread, salads, wraps, or the toasts of your choice. My favorite way to serve this egg salad is on toasted English muffins, but the egg salad is also delicious on its own.

6 eggs

1 to 2 chipotle peppers in adobo sauce, finely minced

3 tbsp (45 g) mayonnaise

1 tsp fresh lime juice

½ tsp kosher salt

⅛ tsp freshly ground black or cayenne pepper

⅛ tsp ground cumin

Pinch of smoked or plain paprika

Chives, freshly minced (optional)

3 to 4 English muffins, toasted

Place the eggs in a small saucepan and cover with water. Cover the pan with a lid and bring the water to a boil. When the water is at a rolling boil, turn off the heat but do not remove the lid. Set a timer for 18 minutes. Drain the water and cool the eggs under cold water. Peel the eggs.

Chop and smash the eggs. Place them in a small mixing bowl. Add the peppers, mayonnaise, lime juice, salt, pepper, cumin, and paprika to the bowl with the eggs. Stir to combine. Taste and adjust the seasonings and peppers as needed. Sprinkle with fresh chives, if desired. Scoop the egg salad onto the toasted English muffins.

Cook's Note: I love this recipe exactly as written, and I always use two chipotle peppers when I make this. While we don't find it very spicy, I recommend starting with just one pepper and then adjusting for your tastes if you're leery of the heat.

BREAKFAST CARBONARA

Yield:
4 servings

Pasta for breakfast? Oh, yes, this is a favorite in my family. Coated with a creamy egg sauce, this easy breakfast is likely to become a favorite in your house as well. This quick and easy version of pasta carbonara is one that I will happily eat without any meat at all. However, if you happen to have some sausage or bacon in the house, it makes a great addition to this breakfast.

1 tbsp (17 g) kosher salt

8 oz (228 g) thin spaghetti

1 tbsp (14 g) butter or oil

2 cloves garlic, minced

½ cup (67 g) frozen green peas

2 eggs, lightly beaten

¼ cup (20 g) freshly grated Parmesan or pecorino Romano cheese

¼ cup (10 g) fresh Italian parsley, chopped

Bring a large pot of water and salt to a boil. Add the pasta and cook until tender.

While the pasta is cooking, heat the butter in a large skillet over medium heat. Add the garlic and the peas and cook, stirring constantly, for 2 minutes. Use tongs to transfer the cooked pasta directly from the water to the skillet. Save the pasta water. Toss the pasta with the peas and the oil. Pour the eggs over the hot pasta and continue tossing to coat the pasta with the eggs. Remove from the heat. Sprinkle with cheese and parsley. Add a splash of the hot pasta water (about 2 to 3 tablespoons [30 to 45 ml]) if the pasta looks dry. Taste the pasta and add salt, if needed.

Cook's Note: If you are unfamiliar with cooking carbonara, rest assured that the hot pasta will cook the egg as it is being tossed, and it will form a great sauce.

TORTILLA EGGS

Yield:
1 serving

This is my middle son's favorite breakfast right now. It's our take on the classic egg-in-a-hole minus the hole, because the egg cooks on the tortilla rather than in it. The whole family loves these Tortilla Eggs. We especially like this with a soft egg, but it also works well with a firmer egg.

1 tsp butter

1 egg

¼ tsp Crazy Salt Seasoning Mix (page 184)

2 tbsp (16 g) shredded Mexican cheese blend, divided

1 (6-inch [15-cm]) flour tortilla

OPTIONAL TOPPINGS
Green onions

Fresh cilantro

Hot sauce or salsa

Melt the butter in a large skillet over medium-high heat. Add an egg and sprinkle with Crazy Salt. Cook until the egg turns white throughout, about 1 minute. Reduce the heat to medium. Flip the egg over, sprinkle with 1 tablespoon (8 g) of cheese, and top with a tortilla. Cook for 1 minute.

Carefully slide a spatula underneath the egg. Flip over so the tortilla is on the bottom and sprinkle the egg with 1 tablespoon (8 g) of cheese. Cover with a lid, reduce the heat to medium, and cook for 1 minute, until the cheese melts. Slide onto a plate, and top with green onions, cilantro, and hot sauce or salsa, if desired.

Cook's Note: Salt and pepper may be substituted for the Crazy Salt in this recipe.

CHEESY EGG FRENCH BREAD BREAKFAST PIZZA

Yield:
6 to 8
servings

This cheesy breakfast pizza comes together in about twenty minutes, not much longer than the time required to scramble the eggs and melt the cheese. If you're lucky enough to have any leftover slices, they store nicely in an airtight container in the refrigerator and reheat well in the microwave or toaster oven.

1 loaf French bread

1 cup (113 g) shredded Monterey Jack cheese, divided

1 cup (120 g) shredded cheddar cheese, divided

10 eggs

2 tbsp (30 ml) water

1 tbsp (14 g) butter

1 tsp Crazy Salt Seasoning Mix (page 184) or store-bought all-purpose seasoning

2 tbsp (5 g) chives or green onions, minced or finely sliced

Cholula hot sauce (optional)

Preheat the oven to 350°F (177°).

Slice the bread in half horizontally, then slice each side of bread into 3 to 4 large pieces. Arrange the bread cut side up on a large baking tray. Mix the cheeses together, and then sprinkle the bread with half the cheese.

Break the eggs into a large mixing bowl. Add the water to the eggs and whisk to combine. In a large skillet over medium-high heat, melt the butter and swirl to coat. Pour the egg mixture into the middle of the pan (you want the butter to move to the edges of the eggs in the pan), and cook without stirring for 1 to 2 minutes. Sprinkle the eggs with Crazy Salt. Once the eggs begin to set, gently stir or fold the eggs as needed until the liquid is almost completely gone. Remove the skillet from the heat while the eggs are still slightly wet.

Gently break up the eggs and scoop them onto the sections of bread. Top the eggs with the remaining cheese.

Bake the pizza until the cheese has melted and the edges of the bread are lightly browned, approximately 4 to 6 minutes. Remove the tray from the oven and sprinkle the pizza with chives before serving. Serve with hot sauce drizzled on top, if desired.

Cook's Notes: Choose a relatively flat loaf of bread, not an especially round one. I like to pick it up the night before I'm planning to make the pizza so it's nice and fresh. If the only bread available is especially round, I recommend hollowing it out a bit after you have sliced it. Simply remove a small amount of the fluffy interior, making it a more balanced amount of toppings and crust.

You can substitute ¾ teaspoon of kosher salt and ½ teaspoon of freshly ground black pepper for the Crazy Salt in this recipe.

TOMATO AND GOAT CHEESE SKILLET SOUFFLÉ

<table>
<tr><td>Yield:
3 to 4
servings</td><td>Fluffy soufflé with fresh tomatoes and creamy goat cheese is a light and tasty breakfast that sounds much fancier than it actually is. The soufflé will cook in about ten minutes, and the only real prep time involved is a quick beating of the egg whites before stirring everything together.

Unlike most of the other recipes in this book, the soufflé will not hold well in the refrigerator. If you don't anticipate eating all of it, I recommend cooking a half recipe in a smaller 6-inch (15-cm) skillet.</td></tr>
</table>

6 eggs

¼ cup (12 g) fresh chives, minced

½ tsp kosher salt

¼ to ½ tsp freshly ground black pepper

1 tbsp (14 g) butter

10 grape tomatoes, halved

2 oz (56 g) crumbled goat cheese

Preheat the oven to 400°F (204°C).

Separate the egg yolks into a large mixing bowl. Place the egg whites in a separate mixing bowl. Whisk the chives, salt, and pepper together with the yolks. Using an electric mixer, beat the whites on low for about 1 minute, until foamy. Increase the speed to medium-high and beat the whites until firm white peaks form, about 3 to 4 minutes. Gently stir the whites into the egg yolks with a spatula.

Melt the butter in a 10- to 12-inch (25- to 30-cm) nonstick skillet over medium heat. Use a spatula to make sure the butter coats the entire pan. Remove from the heat. Pour the egg mixture into the skillet. Scatter the tomatoes and the goat cheese across the top. Bake for 10 minutes, until fluffy and cooked through.

SLOW COOKER RAISIN NUT OATMEAL

Yield:
4 servings

Slow cooker oatmeal may not sound like a quick and easy breakfast, but I promise you that it is. If you start the oatmeal when you start your coffee, it should be done cooking by the time you are dressed and ready to eat. You'll have a stress-free, no-fuss hot breakfast on the table with less than five minutes' effort.

Depending on how long you cook this oatmeal, it can be served thick like stove top oatmeal or with soft oats and warm milk, muesli-style; it's delicious both ways. This is an oatmeal that my whole family enjoys.

2 cups (312 g) old-fashioned rolled oats

½ cup (55 g) pecans or walnuts, chopped

⅓ cup (48 g) raisins, assorted varieties work great

3 tbsp (38 g) brown sugar

1 tsp ground cinnamon

½ tsp ground nutmeg

½ tsp kosher salt

3 cups (710 ml) milk

OPTIONAL TOPPINGS
Sliced bananas

Berries

Cream

Add the oats, pecans, raisins, brown sugar, cinnamon, nutmeg, salt, and milk to the slow cooker. Stir to combine. Cover and cook on high for 30 minutes to 1 hour, or on low for 2 hours. Add toppings, if desired.

Cook's Notes: Avoid lifting the lid to check the oatmeal. Each time the lid is lifted, it adds to the cooking time. This recipe doubles nicely for more servings; however, it will thicken significantly in the refrigerator. I don't recommend making extra for another day.

Depending on the size of your slow cooker and how hot it gets at different settings, this oatmeal might cook in as quickly as 30 minutes or take as long as 90 minutes to cook. I recommend making this for the first time on a weekend when you don't need it ready at a specific time. Once you know how you like it and how long it takes to cook, you'll be able to plan well for busy mornings.

CAPRESE OMELET

Yield:
1 to 2
servings

A few eggs, fresh tomato, a sprinkling of cheese, and fresh basil are combined to make this flavorful omelet. This breakfast comes together in minutes and my whole family loves it.

3 eggs

1 tbsp (15 ml) water

1 tsp olive oil

¼ tsp kosher salt

¼ tsp freshly ground black pepper

2 oz (56 g) mozzarella, thinly sliced, torn, or shredded

1 roma tomato, cut into ¼-inch (6-mm) slices

4 basil leaves, sliced into thin ribbons

Whisk the eggs with the water in a small bowl. Heat a medium-size nonstick skillet over medium-high heat. Drizzle with oil and pour the eggs into the skillet. Sprinkle with salt and pepper. Let the eggs cook without touching them until they set around the edges and are slightly bubbling, about 2 minutes. There should be very little liquid at this point.

Use a large spatula to carefully and quickly flip the eggs over like a giant pancake. Reduce the heat to low. Working quickly, add half the cheese, tomato, and basil to one half of the eggs in the skillet. Sprinkle the tomato with the remaining cheese and fold the egg over on itself. Cover the skillet with a lid and cook just long enough to melt the cheese, about 1 to 2 minutes. Serve immediately.

BREAKFAST TOSTADA STACKS

Yield:
3 servings

Crisp tostada shells, creamy refried beans, cheese, and a soft fried egg are stacked to create these breakfast tostadas. This is a fun breakfast that my kids have gone nuts over. Luckily, this recipe comes together in just about ten minutes, making it perfect for busy mornings too.

6 crispy tostada shells

1 (16-oz [454-g]) can refried beans

1 cup (130 g) shredded Colby Jack or pepper Jack cheese

1 tbsp (14 g) butter, divided

3 eggs

Salt and pepper

2 tbsp (30 ml) water, divided

1 green onion, thinly sliced

1 tbsp (1 g) fresh cilantro, minced

2 tbsp (19 g) Cotija cheese, crumbled (optional)

Preheat the oven to 350°F (177°C).

Place the tostada shells on a large baking sheet. Stir the beans until smooth and then divide them onto each of the tostada shells. Spread the beans across the shells with a spatula. Sprinkle the shredded cheese over each tostada. Bake until the cheese melts, about 5 to 8 minutes.

While the tostadas are baking, melt ½ tablespoon (7 g) of butter in a large nonstick skillet over medium-low heat. When the butter begins to foam, tilt the pan to coat the bottom with butter. Add 2 eggs to the skillet. When the edges of the eggs turn white, season them lightly with salt and pepper. Add 1 tablespoon (15 ml) of water to the pan and cover it with a lid. Remove the eggs from the heat when they're still soft and runny. Slide the cooked eggs onto a plate and tent them with foil. Drain any liquid from the pan and add ½ tablespoon (7 g) of butter to the hot skillet. Repeat the steps with the remaining egg.

When the cheese on the tostadas has melted, place 3 of them on plates and stack another tostada on top. Place an egg on top of each stack and sprinkle with onion, cilantro, and Cotija cheese, if desired.

Cook's Note: Soft corn tortillas may be substituted for the crispy tostada shells. If you aren't a fan of Cotija cheese, feel free to substitute a sprinkling of your favorite cheese.

SAVORY OATMEAL WITH MUSHROOMS AND EGG

Yield:
4 servings

If you're like the rest of my family was initially, the thought of oatmeal being savory is throwing you a bit. I promise, though, if you will give it a try, this oatmeal just might change your mind. My kids were skeptical at first, but after that first bite I had three new fans of savory oatmeal. The creamy oats topped with an egg and the garlicky mushrooms absolutely works. Add a splash of hot sauce and you might find yourself in breakfast heaven.

2 cups (160 g) old-fashioned rolled oats

3½ cups (830 ml) low-sodium chicken broth

½ tsp freshly ground black pepper, divided

1 tsp olive oil

2 cloves garlic, minced

8 large mushrooms, thinly sliced, about 2 cups (132 g)

½ tsp kosher salt

1 tbsp (14 g) butter, divided

4 eggs

1 tbsp (15 ml) water

2 green onions, thinly sliced (optional)

Cholula or alternate hot sauce (optional)

Combine the oats, chicken broth, and ¼ teaspoon of black pepper in a small saucepan. Bring to a boil. Reduce the heat to simmer and cook until the oats are tender and the liquid has been mostly absorbed, about 3 minutes. Remove from the heat.

While the oatmeal is simmering, warm the oil in a large skillet over medium-high heat. Add the garlic and mushrooms. Cook, stirring occasionally, until the mushrooms are tender. Season with salt and the remaining black pepper. Transfer the mushrooms to a plate.

Melt the butter in a large nonstick skillet over medium-low heat. When the butter begins to foam, tilt the pan to coat the bottom with butter. Add 2 eggs to the skillet. When the edges of the eggs turn white, season lightly with salt and pepper. Add 1 tablespoon (15 ml) of water to the pan and cover with a lid. Remove them from the heat when they're still soft and runny. Slide the cooked eggs onto a plate and tent them with foil. Drain any liquid from the pan and add ½ tablespoon (7 g) of butter to the hot skillet. Repeat the steps with 1 to 2 more eggs.

Scoop the oatmeal into bowls. Top with mushrooms and an egg. Sprinkle with green onions and drizzle with hot sauce, if desired.

Cook's Note: This oatmeal can also be made with quick-cooking steel-cut oats, if that's more your style. Follow the package directions for cooking the oats (substitute broth for the water), and then proceed with the recipe.

FANCY BREAKFAST TOASTS

Yield:
1 serving

For the days when you have just a few minutes to pull together a bite to eat, these toasts are here to save your morning. Peanut butter with sliced bananas has been my go-to breakfast toast ever since I was a kid, and this dressed-up version is even more fun. Both the kids and the adults in our house have given thumbs-up approval to each of these combinations. My current favorite is the blueberry and basil toast. My kids go for the prosciutto anytime it is in the house.

Depending on your breakfast appetite, a slice or two of toast will be plenty for most people. Most mornings 1 slice is perfect for me; however, my boys like to make a couple of slices for themselves.

1 slice hearty bread (whole grain or multigrain)

SWEET AND SALTY PEANUT BUTTER BANANA TOAST
1 tbsp (16 g) smooth peanut butter

½ banana, thinly sliced

1 tsp honey

Pinch of kosher salt (optional)

1 tsp sliced almonds

CREAM CHEESE AND PEPPER JAM TOAST
2 tbsp (48 g) whipped cream cheese

2 tsp (4 g) sweet and spicy pepper jam, fig also works nicely

1 to 2 slices prosciutto, folded and crumpled

AVOCADO TOAST
2 tsp (10 g) butter

¼ to ½ avocado, sliced very thin

Pinch of kosher salt

Pinch of freshly ground black pepper

Favorite hot sauce, drizzle

TOMATO GOAT CHEESE TOAST
2 tbsp (19 g) goat cheese

1 tomato, thinly sliced

Kosher salt

Freshly ground black pepper

2 leaves fresh basil, thinly sliced

Balsamic vinegar, drizzle

BLUEBERRY BASIL CREAM CHEESE TOAST
2 tbsp (48 g) whipped cream cheese or goat cheese

¼ cup (37 g) fresh blueberries

2 leaves basil, torn or thinly sliced

1 tsp honey

Toast the bread and then layer with your favorite combination of ingredients in the order listed.

Make-Ahead Breakfasts

These recipes are some of my favorite breakfasts, and like the chapter title says, they all can be made ahead of time and stashed in the refrigerator and freezer. Whether you have time in the morning for a little bit more prep, or you're making these on the weekend for breakfasts during the week, the recipes are all simple ones that are sure to become favorites in your home as well.

Savory French Toast Bake (page 139) is filled with chunks of ham and cheese. It's perfect straight out of the oven or reheated a day or two later. Scrambled Sliders (page 136) are almost too simple to be so delicious, but they are. I make a double batch of the sliders at least every other month, and the kids ask for them frequently.

Are you looking for a low-carb high-protein breakfast that will reheat well? Cheesy Bacon and Spinach Egg Cups (page 148) are a staple in our freezer. Or does breakfast require something sweet in your house? If so, Grandma's Waffles with Waffle Sauce (page 147) freeze beautifully and are guaranteed to make a weekday morning special.

Last but not least, the Cheddar, Chive, and Sausage Biscuits (page 140) have been one of the most popular recipes in this book. I keep them on hand for breakfasts and for snacking throughout the day.

BLACKBERRY ALMOND BAKED OATMEAL

Tart blackberries and crisp almonds are the stars in this recipe; however, baked oatmeal is incredibly versatile, so feel free to swap the berries for raisins, cranberries, or peaches, and trade the almonds for pecans or walnuts. Choose your favorite flavor combination and make it your own. Baked oatmeal is a favorite breakfast in our family. I love having portions tucked away in the freezer for the busiest of mornings.

3½ cups (282 g) old-fashioned rolled oats

⅓ cup (67 g) light brown sugar

2 tsp (9 g) baking powder

1 tsp kosher salt

1 tsp ground cinnamon

¼ cup (60 ml) light flavored olive oil

3 eggs

1½ cups (355 ml) milk

6 oz (170 g) fresh blackberries or blueberries*

½ cup (46 g) sliced almonds, divided*

Fresh whipped cream, for topping (optional)

* ALTERNATIVE ADD-INS
½ cup (55 g) chopped pecans plus ¾ cup (90 g) craisins or dried cranberries

1½ cups (231 g) very thinly sliced fresh peaches

½ cup (63 g) walnuts plus ¾ cup (109 g) raisins

Preheat the oven to 350°F (177°C).

Grease a 9 × 13-inch (23 × 33-cm) pan with butter or coat with cooking spray. Add the oats, brown sugar, baking powder, salt, and cinnamon in a large mixing bowl. Stir to combine. Whisk together the oil, eggs, and milk in a separate bowl. Add the wet ingredients to the dry ingredients, and stir to combine. Stir in the blackberries and half of the almonds or the alternative add-ins of your choice.

Scoop the oat mixture into the greased pan and sprinkle with the remaining almonds. Bake for 30 minutes. The oatmeal should be lightly browned around the edges and slightly crisp on top. A knife inserted will come out mostly clean with wet crumbs. Remove from the oven and let cool for 10 minutes before serving. Slice into servings or scoop out servings with a spoon. Top with whipped cream, if desired.

MAKE-AHEAD DIRECTIONS
Let the oatmeal cool completely and then cut or scoop into portions. Store in an airtight container in the refrigerator for up to 3 days. Reheat in the microwave or covered in the oven. This can be stored in one large container or portioned into individual servings for storage and reheating. Before reheating individual portions in the microwave, add 1 tablespoon (15 ml) of water to the container.

SCRAMBLED SLIDERS

Yield:
24 sliders,
about 12 to
24 servings

A kid favorite and an adult favorite for a while now, these sliders are my family's first choice for breakfast anytime they are in the freezer. Filled with cheesy eggs and bites of bacon or sausage, they freeze beautifully and reheat well. They're great for making sure everyone has a hearty hot breakfast, even on the busiest of mornings. While I typically eat just one slider, my husband and kids often eat two.

1 lb (454 g) breakfast sausage or bacon, cooked and crumbled

18 eggs

¼ cup (60 ml) water

1 tbsp (14 g) butter

1 tsp Crazy Salt Seasoning Mix (page 184) or store-bought all-purpose seasoning

4 oz (113 g) freshly shredded medium cheddar cheese

24 slider rolls

Cook and crumble the sausage or bacon in a very large skillet over medium-high heat, about 5 minutes. Transfer the cooked meat to a plate. Drain any grease from the skillet.

Break the eggs into a large mixing bowl. Add the water to the eggs and whisk to combine. Place the skillet back over medium-high heat and add the butter. Swirl to coat as it melts. Pour the egg mixture into the middle of the pan (you want the butter to move to the edges of the eggs in the pan) and cook without stirring for a minute or two. Sprinkle with Crazy Salt.

Once the eggs begin to set, gently stir or fold the eggs as needed until the liquid is almost completely gone. Remove the skillet from the heat while the eggs are still slightly wet.

Add the meat back to the skillet and stir gently to break up the eggs and distribute the meat throughout. Sprinkle with cheese, and stir gently to melt the cheese.

Open the slider rolls and set the bottom halves on a large tray. Divide the eggs on top of the rolls and place the top half of the rolls over the eggs.

Serve immediately or follow the make-ahead directions for storage.

MAKE-AHEAD DIRECTIONS
Place the sandwiches in a zip-top freezer bag or in an airtight container. Sandwiches may be stored in the refrigerator for up to 3 days. Reheat individual sandwiches wrapped in a paper towel in the microwave. Sandwiches can also be reheated on a tray covered with foil in the oven.

ALTERNATIVE MAKE-AHEAD DIRECTIONS
Store the scrambled egg and sausage mixture in an airtight container in the refrigerator for up to 3 days. Reheat in the microwave or on the stove, and fill the slider rolls when ready to eat.

SAVORY FRENCH TOAST BAKE

Yield:
5 to 6
servings

As much as I love classic French toast with maple syrup, I prefer a savory breakfast most of the time. However, the convenience of a French toast casserole cannot be beat. This is my take on a classic French toast casserole made savory with salty ham, gooey cheese, and a handful of fresh vegetables.

1 loaf French bread

6 eggs

½ cup (120 ml) milk

½ cup (119 g) heavy cream

½ tsp kosher salt

½ tsp freshly ground black pepper

½ tsp granulated garlic or garlic powder

½ lb (227 g) fresh asparagus, trimmed and cut into 1-inch (2.5-cm) pieces

½ lb (227 g) thinly sliced deli ham, chopped into 1-inch (2.5-cm) pieces

1½ cups (195 g) shredded Swiss cheese, divided

Preheat the oven to 350°F (177°C).

Grease a 9 × 13-inch (23 × 33-cm) baking dish and set aside. Use a sharp knife to slice the bread into 1-inch (2.5-cm)-thick pieces, and then cut those pieces into 1-inch (2.5-cm) cubes. Place the bread in a large mixing bowl.

In a small bowl, lightly whisk the eggs and add the milk, cream, salt, pepper, and garlic. Whisk to combine, and pour the liquid over the bread cubes. Use a large spoon to gently stir and coat all the bread cubes. Add the asparagus, ham, and 1 cup (130 g) of shredded cheese. Toss once more to evenly distribute the ingredients.

Transfer the mixture to the prepared baking dish and make sure the ham and asparagus are distributed throughout. Sprinkle with the remaining cheese. Cover with foil and bake for 30 minutes. Remove the foil and bake for 20 to 22 minutes uncovered. The bread should be toasted golden brown. Remove from the oven and serve warm. Store any leftovers in the refrigerator.

MAKE-AHEAD DIRECTIONS
Store this in an airtight container in the refrigerator for up to 3 days. Reheat in the microwave or covered in the oven. This can be stored in one large container or portioned into individual servings for storage and reheating.

Cook's Note: If you don't happen to be a fan of asparagus, this works nicely with broccoli or bell peppers as well.

CHEDDAR, CHIVE, AND SAUSAGE BISCUITS

<table>
<tr><td>Yield:
12 large or 18
medium-size
biscuits</td><td>Light and fluffy, cheddar and sausage biscuits are made with cornmeal for extra flavor. They're sprinkled throughout with fresh chives and baked until golden. These drop biscuits are a great grab-and-go breakfast option.

They freeze nicely and reheat in the microwave in under a minute. My kids love these for breakfasts and for snacking. Typically, we eat them on their own, but they also make a great hearty breakfast alongside eggs.</td></tr>
</table>

½ lb (227 g) breakfast or country sausage

1 cup (230 g) sour cream

2 eggs

¼ cup (60 ml) butter, melted

1¼ cups (156 g) all-purpose flour*

¾ cup (119 g) cornmeal

¼ cup (50 g) sugar

2 tsp (9 g) baking powder

1 tsp kosher salt

1½ cups (181 g) sharp cheddar cheese, freshly shredded

⅓ cup (17 g) chives, finely minced

* GLUTEN-FREE ALTERNATIVE
¾ cup (119 g) brown rice flour

⅓ cup (35 g) tapioca starch

2 tbsp (22 g) potato starch

½ tsp xanthan gum

In a large skillet over medium-high heat, cook and crumble the sausage. Remove from the heat, drain any grease, and let cool.

Preheat the oven to 400°F (204°C).

In a large mixing bowl, whisk together the sour cream and eggs. Add the butter and whisk again to combine. Add the flour, cornmeal, sugar, baking powder, and salt to the bowl. Stir to combine.

Add the cooked sausage, cheese, and chives to the batter. Stir to mix thoroughly. Scoop and drop the batter onto a parchment-lined sheet pan. The biscuits will not rise much, and they shouldn't spread, so they will easily fit on one tray. Bake the smaller biscuits for 14 to 16 minutes, and bake the larger ones for 24 to 26 minutes, until lightly browned.

MAKE-AHEAD DIRECTIONS
Store the biscuits in an airtight container in the refrigerator for up to 3 days. Serve at room temperature or reheat in the microwave or covered in the oven. These biscuits can also be frozen for up to 2 months. Thaw at room temperature or in the refrigerator. Reheat as desired.

Cook's Notes: For this recipe, it's important to use freshly shredded cheese. Preshredded store-bought varieties won't melt into the muffins the same way.

Green onions will also work in this recipe if chives are not available.

MAKE-AHEAD FRUIT AND NUT OATMEAL

Yield:
10 to 12
servings

The beauty of this oatmeal is that you can make it on the stove or in the microwave in very little time. Stir together a big batch, and you'll have breakfast ready in under two minutes on the busiest of mornings.

6 cups (483 g) old-fashioned rolled oats

1 cup (109 g) chopped pecans

¾ cup (94 g) chopped walnuts

¾ cup (69 g) sliced almonds

1½ cups (300 g) dried fruits, any variety, chopped small as needed

½ to 1 cup (47 to 93 g) sweetened shredded coconut (optional)

½ cup (100 g) light brown sugar

2 tbsp (16 g) ground cinnamon

2 tsp (5 g) ground nutmeg

3 tsp (12 g) kosher salt

In a large mixing bowl, place the oats, pecans, walnuts, almonds, dried fruits, coconut, brown sugar, cinnamon, nutmeg, and salt. Stir to combine. Store in an airtight container for up to 3 weeks.

STOVE TOP DIRECTIONS FOR 1 SERVING
Combine 1 cup (154 g) of the oatmeal mixture and 1½ cups (355 ml) of water in a pot on the stove. Bring to a boil. Reduce to simmer and cook until the water has been absorbed and the oats are soft, about 5 minutes.

MICROWAVE DIRECTIONS FOR 1 SERVING
Place 1 cup (154 g) of the oatmeal mixture in a glass bowl along with ½ to ¾ cup (120 to 180 ml) of water. Microwave for 90 to 120 seconds, stir, and then let it rest for at least 2 minutes before serving.

Adjust the liquid and the cooking time according to your preference. I like my oatmeal more chewy than soft, so ½ cup (120 ml) of water and 90 seconds works for me. My boys like theirs a little softer, so ¾ cup (180 ml) of water and 120 seconds works for them.

Cook's Note: Adjust the sugar according to your preference. I found that the dried fruits made it plenty sweet for our tastes. Our favorite dried fruit combination is apricots (chopped very small) and an assortment of raisins (currants, golden seedless, sultanas, and traditional natural seedless raisins).

CAJUN POTATO BREAKFAST CASSEROLE

Yield:
8 servings

This is a fluffy, hearty breakfast casserole that only takes a few minutes to stir together. My kids love this breakfast, and it easily makes enough for a couple of busy mornings. As an added bonus, it freezes nicely too, so feel free to double the recipe and stash a pan in the freezer. Thaw it in the refrigerator overnight and just reheat in the morning.

8 eggs

1 cup (229 g) cottage cheese

4 green onions, thinly sliced, about ⅓ cup (17 g)

1 small green bell pepper, chopped into ½-inch (1-cm) pieces, about 1 cup (149 g)

1 tbsp (3 g) Cajun Seasoning Mix (page 184) or see Cook's Notes

20 oz (567 g) refrigerated shredded hash brown potatoes

2 cups (260 g) shredded Mexican blend cheese, divided

Chopped fresh cilantro or green onions, sliced thin (optional)

Preheat the oven to 350°F (177°C).

Lightly grease a 9 × 13-inch (23 × 33-cm) pan with oil or butter. In a large mixing bowl, lightly beat the eggs. Add the cottage cheese, green onions, bell pepper, and Cajun seasoning. Whisk to combine. Add the hash browns and 1½ cups (195 g) of cheese. Stir to mix thoroughly.

Pour the egg mixture into the greased casserole dish. Top with the remaining cheese. Bake until lightly browned, about 50 to 55 minutes. Sprinkle with cilantro or additional green onions before serving, if desired.

MAKE-AHEAD DIRECTIONS
Store this in an airtight container in the refrigerator for up to 3 days. Reheat in the microwave or covered in the oven. This can be stored in one large container or portioned into individual servings for storage and reheating.

Cook's Notes: Frozen hash browns can be substituted for the refrigerated ones. Simply increase the cooking time by 10 to 15 minutes. This casserole is also great with 1 pound (454 g) of cooked and crumbled bacon or sausage stirred in along with the hash browns.

The following combination of spices may be substituted for the Cajun spice mix listed in the recipe:

¾ tsp smoked or plain paprika

¾ tsp granulated garlic or garlic powder

½ tsp granulated onion or onion powder

½ tsp kosher salt

½ tsp freshly ground black pepper

½ tsp dried oregano

¼ tsp dried thyme

¼ tsp cayenne pepper

GRANDMA'S WAFFLES WITH WAFFLE SAUCE

Yield:
5 full-size Belgian waffles

Light and fluffy waffles that are crisp on the outside and tender inside are a year-round favorite in our house. My family has been making waffles along with my grandma's waffle sauce since long before I was born. I was happy to discover that both the waffles and the sauce freeze beautifully, making this a dream of a make-ahead breakfast.

The added starches in the gluten-free version of this recipe make them extra crisp on the outside. I might be guilty of loving the gluten-free recipe even more than Grandma's original, but truly they are both delicious.

WAFFLES
2 cups (250 g) all-purpose flour*

1 tsp kosher salt

1½ tbsp (21 g) baking powder

1 tbsp (13 g) sugar

1⅔ cups (400 ml) milk

2 eggs

⅓ cup (80 ml) butter, melted

1 tsp vanilla extract

* GLUTEN-FREE ALTERNATIVE
1⅓ cups (211 g) brown rice flour

⅔ cup (69 g) tapioca starch

¼ cup (44 g) potato starch

WAFFLE SAUCE
¼ cup (31 g) all-purpose flour**

¾ cup (150 g) sugar

2 cups (474 ml) milk

2 tbsp (30 g) butter

1 tsp vanilla extract

½ tsp freshly ground nutmeg, if possible, or store-bought ground nutmeg

** GLUTEN-FREE ALTERNATIVE
¼ cup (40 g) brown rice flour

Preheat the waffle iron.

In a medium-size mixing bowl, combine the flour, salt, baking powder, and sugar. Add the milk and the eggs. Whisk to combine. Pour the melted butter and the vanilla into the batter and whisk until mostly smooth.

Pour the batter onto the hot waffle iron and cook according to manufacturer's directions. Serve warm.

For the waffle sauce, combine the flour and sugar in a small saucepan over medium-high heat. Whisk to combine. Add the milk and whisk well to combine. Cook, whisking frequently, until thickened, about 5 minutes. Remove from the heat. Stir in the butter and vanilla. Pour the sauce over the waffles and sprinkle with nutmeg.

MAKE-AHEAD DIRECTIONS
Completely cool the waffles and store in zip-top bags in the refrigerator for up to 3 days or in the freezer for up to 2 months. Reheat in the toaster, in the microwave, or covered in the oven. Store the waffle sauce in an airtight container in the refrigerator for up to 3 days or in the freezer for up to 2 months. This can be stored in one large container or portioned into individual servings for storage. Thaw the waffle sauce and reheat on the stove or in the microwave.

CHEESY BACON AND SPINACH EGG CUPS

Yield:
6 servings

Eggs baked with bacon, spinach, and a sprinkling of cheese are a tasty low-carb breakfast recipe that I make frequently. I like to keep these egg cups in the freezer for the mornings when I want a healthy breakfast and simply don't have more than a minute to cook something.

10 eggs

¼ cup (60 ml) milk

1 tsp Crazy Salt Seasoning Mix (page 184) or store-bought all-purpose seasoning

1 tbsp (15 g) butter, to grease the muffin tins

1 cup (45 g) finely chopped baby spinach leaves

½ lb (227 g) bacon, cooked and chopped small (optional)

3 oz (85 g) cheddar, Monterey Jack, or pepper Jack cheese, shredded

Preheat the oven to 350°F (177°C).

In a large mixing bowl, whisk together the eggs, milk, and Crazy Salt.

Grease a 12-cup muffin tin very thoroughly with butter. Pour a scant ¼ cup (56 g) of the egg mixture into each muffin tin, distributing as evenly as possible. Drop 1 tablespoon (2 g) of spinach and several pieces of crumbled bacon in each and stir to mix. Top with a light sprinkling of cheese.

Bake for 20 to 22 minutes, until the eggs are cooked through and the tops are lightly browned. They will be puffy and rounded when they come out of the oven and will sink back to level as they rest.

MAKE-AHEAD DIRECTIONS
Store in an airtight container or zip-top bag in the refrigerator for up to 3 days or in the freezer for up to 2 months. Reheat in the microwave or covered in the oven. These can be stored in one large container or portioned into individual servings for storage and reheating.

Cook's Note: These egg cups also work well with cooked and crumbled sausage or diced ham. I've made this recipe with store-bought precooked bacon, and it works fine. Simply chop 4 ounces (114 g) of store-bought precooked bacon and add it directly to the recipe.

PERFECT PANCAKES

Yield:
18 to 20
medium
pancakes

Light and fluffy pancakes are a breakfast favorite. I like to make a giant batch on the weekend and freeze them for easy breakfasts through the week. Topped with peanut butter and maple syrup, berries and whipped cream, butter and fruit jams or spreads, these pancakes are a breakfast that everyone loves. I frequently triple this recipe for my family, so we'll have plenty in the freezer for easy breakfasts.

2½ cups (313 g) all-purpose flour*

2 tbsp (28 g) baking powder

2 tbsp (25 g) sugar

1 tsp salt

2 cups (474 ml) milk**

2 eggs

2 tbsp (30 ml) butter, melted and cooled

* GLUTEN-FREE ALTERNATIVE

1¾ cups (277 g) brown rice flour

½ cup (52 g) tapioca starch

½ cup (87 g) potato starch

** *When making these pancakes GF, reduce the milk to 1½ cups (355 ml).*

Stir together the flour, baking powder, sugar, and salt. Add the milk and the eggs to the dry ingredients. Whisk to combine, and then add the butter. Whisk some more, and then let the batter rest while the griddle or pan heats.

Heat a flat-bottom nonstick skillet or electric griddle over medium heat. Butter the skillet or griddle lightly and then pour a scant ¼ cup (59 g) of batter onto the griddle for each pancake. Let cook until they begin to bubble on top and are lightly browned on the bottom. Flip and cook the second side just until golden brown. Serve warm with the toppings of your choice.

MAKE-AHEAD DIRECTIONS

Store the completely cooled pancakes in an airtight container or in zip-top bags in the refrigerator for up to 3 days or in the freezer for up to 2 months. Reheat in the microwave, in the toaster, or covered in the oven.

Cook's Notes: I adore blueberry pancakes and more often than not (basically anytime I can get my hands on fresh blueberries) I add them to the pancakes. To make sure each pancake has a great number of berries, I like to add the berries after pouring the batter on the griddle. Scatter 8 to 10 berries over the top of the bubbling pancakes before flipping them over.

If chocolate chip pancakes are more your style, sprinkle chocolate chips across the bubbling pancakes in place of the blueberries above.

CHRISTMAS BREAKFAST ENCHILADA CASSEROLE

Yield:
6 servings

When you order food in New Mexico, you are often asked, "Red or green?" It's jokingly called the state motto. It refers to red and green chile. A Christmas plate is what you request if you want both red and green. These enchiladas combine the best of both worlds. We share a love for both red and green chiles in my family, so we enjoy this recipe Christmas-style by making half the pan with red sauce on top and the other half with green sauce.

This is a great make-ahead breakfast. I like to make and bake these enchiladas, and then my kids can serve themselves and reheat portions through the week.

½ lb (227 g) breakfast sausage, regular or spicy

½ small onion, diced into ½-inch (13-mm) pieces, about ½ cup (80 g)

1 small red or green bell pepper, diced into ½-inch (13-mm) pieces, about ¾ cup (112 g)

1 (4-oz [114-g]) can chopped green chile, hot or mild

10 eggs

1 tbsp (14 g) butter

¼ tsp kosher salt

¼ tsp freshly ground black pepper

¼ tsp granulated garlic or garlic powder

1½ cups (355 ml) green or red chile enchilada sauce, or half and half for Christmas-style

5 flour tortillas, or 10 corn tortillas, cut into pie-shaped wedges

5 to 6 cups (565 to 678 g) shredded cheddar, Monterey Jack, or pepper Jack cheese

TOPPINGS (OPTIONAL)
Fresh cilantro

Sour cream

Hot sauce

Preheat the oven to 350°F (177°C).

Crumble the sausage into a large skillet and cook over medium-high heat. As the sausage begins to brown, add the onion and the pepper. Continue cooking, stirring frequently until the vegetables are tender and the meat is fully cooked, about 5 minutes. Add the green chile, and stir to combine.

While the sausage mixture cooks, crack the eggs into a bowl and beat them lightly, just enough to combine them. Transfer the meat and vegetables to a plate and add butter to the skillet over medium-low heat. Pour the eggs into the hot skillet. Season the eggs with salt, pepper, and garlic. As the eggs begin to set, gently pull them across the skillet with a spatula, forming large, soft curds. The eggs are done when they look just a little bit runny. They'll continue to cook a little after you remove them from the heat.

Add the sausage mixture back to the skillet with the eggs. Stir to combine. Pour ½ cup (120 ml) of enchilada sauce (red or green) into the bottom of a 9 × 13-inch (23 × 33-cm) baking dish. Arrange a layer of tortilla wedges over the sauce; distribute half the egg mixture over the tortillas. Sprinkle with 1½ cups (170 g) of cheese. Layer the tortillas over the cheese and then repeat the egg, cheese, and tortilla layers.

Pour the remaining sauce over the top layer of tortillas. Sprinkle generously with the remaining cheese. Bake for 20 to 22 minutes, until the cheese has fully melted and lightly browned. Sprinkle with cilantro and serve with sour cream and hot sauce, if desired.

MAKE-AHEAD DIRECTIONS
Store this in an airtight container in the refrigerator for up to 3 days. Reheat in the microwave or covered in the oven. This casserole can be stored in one large container or portioned into individual servings for storage and reheating. Alternatively, the enchiladas can be prepared the night before without baking and then popped in the oven in the morning. When you're baking it cold from the refrigerator, plan an additional 10 to 15 minutes of cooking time.

SLOW COOKER NUTTY COCONUT GRANOLA

Yield:
12 to 16 servings

When I discovered a few years ago just how easy it is to make granola in the slow cooker, it was a bit of a breakfast game changer. Just dump all the ingredients in the slow cooker, stir a few times, and you're done. Perfect granola every single time at a fraction of the cost of store-bought granola. And guess what? It tastes better than store-bought granola too. This recipe is as adaptable as can be. Play with the flavors. Swap the add-ins with your favorite nuts and dried fruits, and I bet you'll have a new breakfast favorite too.

This granola recipe is a current favorite and I try to keep a batch on hand all the time. I typically make this on a Saturday morning and then keep it in the pantry for easy breakfasts. We make Maple Cinnamon Granola Parfaits (page 110) anytime we have this granola in the house.

½ cup (110 g) coconut oil or butter, divided

5 cups (402 g) old-fashioned rolled oats

¾ cup (82 g) pecans, chopped

¾ cup (69 g) sliced almonds

¾ cup (180 ml) honey

½ tsp kosher salt

½ tsp cinnamon

1 cup (75 g) sweetened coconut flakes

1 cup (120 g) dried cranberries

Set the slow cooker to high. Grease the slow cooker with 1 tablespoon (14 g) of oil. Add the oats, pecans, and almonds to the slow cooker. Combine the honey, remaining coconut oil, salt, and cinnamon in a small glass dish. Microwave for 1 minute. Stir to melt and combine everything. Pour over the oatmeal and nuts in the slow cooker, and stir well to coat.

Cover with the lid, leaving it slightly vented. (I place a chopstick across one end of the slow cooker and set the lid over that.) Cook for 60 to 90 minutes, stirring and scraping the sides and bottom of the slow cooker every 30 minutes. Stir in the coconut and cranberries, and then spread the granola across a large baking sheet. When the granola has cooled, transfer it to an airtight container.

MAKE-AHEAD DIRECTIONS
Store completely cooled granola in an airtight container in the pantry for up to a week. If you live in a humid area, you may want to try storing the granola in the freezer if it softens after a few days. In my climate, this granola stays crunchy at room temperature until it is gone.

Cook's Notes: The cooking time varies depending on how hot your slow cooker gets. This granola averages about 90 minutes for mine. When you begin to smell the granola, it's probably time to stir it again. It is possible to burn the granola in the slow cooker if you do not stir it frequently enough or if you do not scrape the sides and bottom.

The granola is done when the liquids have been absorbed and the oats look moist but not wet. It will finish drying out and clump together a bit while it cools on the baking sheet.

SWEET AND SAVORY HAM AND CHEESE SCONES

Yield:
12 small scones

Lightly sweetened scone meets salty ham and melting cheese in this surprisingly easy scone recipe. My family can't get enough of these each time we make them. This is a small recipe, perfect for any breakfast. It only takes a few minutes to stir them together, so I usually make them fresh the day we eat them. However, these scones do freeze and reheat well. Occasionally, I will make a double batch just to have a few extras tucked in the freezer.

1 cup (125 g) all-purpose flour*

1 tsp baking powder

¼ tsp kosher salt

¼ tsp dried thyme

¼ cup (50 g) raw sugar

¼ cup (57 g) cold butter

⅓ cup (79 ml) plus 1 to 2 tbsp (15 to 30 ml) heavy cream, divided

½ cup (57 g) thinly sliced deli ham

½ cup (57 g) grated cheddar

* GLUTEN-FREE ALTERNATIVES
½ cup (79 g) plus 3 tbsp (38 g) brown rice flour

¼ cup (26 g) tapioca starch

2 tbsp (22 g) potato starch

½ tsp xanthan gum

Preheat the oven to 350°F (177°C).

Line a large baking sheet with parchment. Place the flour, baking powder, salt, thyme, and sugar in a medium-size mixing bowl. Stir with a fork to combine.

Grate the butter and add the butter shreds to the flour mixture. Use the fork to mix the butter into the flour until it's evenly dispersed and approximately pea size.

Add ⅓ cup (79 ml) of cream and stir until a loose dough forms. Chop the ham into very small pieces. Gently fold in the ham and cheese. If the dough is too dry and floury, add just a drizzle more cream until it comes together enough to pinch and mold with your fingers.

Use a 2-tablespoon (30-g) scoop to form 12 round scones on the parchment-lined baking sheet. Bake for 16 to 18 minutes. Transfer the scones to a wire cooling rack and cool completely.

MAKE-AHEAD DIRECTIONS
Store in an airtight container in the refrigerator for up to 3 days. Serve at room temperature or reheat in the microwave or covered in the oven. The scones can also be frozen for up to 2 months. Thaw at room temperature or in the refrigerator. Reheat as desired.

Cook's Note: I've made these scones with several different varieties of thinly sliced meats and shredded cheeses. Pair up your favorite flavor combinations and create your perfect scone.

BLUEBERRY COCONUT CRISP

Yield:
6 servings

Two layers of lightly sweetened coconut and oat streusel surround an abundance of blueberries in this easy crisp recipe. The breakfast crisp is my warm and cozy twist on my family's much-loved Maple Cinnamon Granola Parfaits (page 110). With less added sugar than the more common sweet breakfasts, this is a fun change from the usual choices. This crisp keeps nicely in the refrigerator, making it perfect for warming on a busy morning. Topped with a spoonful of plain yogurt or eaten plain, we absolutely love this breakfast.

FILLING INGREDIENTS
18 oz (511 g) fresh blueberries
¼ cup (50 g) sugar
1 tbsp (8 g) cornstarch
¼ tsp cinnamon

CRISP INGREDIENTS
1 cup (80 g) old-fashioned rolled oats
½ cup (38 g) sweetened flaked coconut
⅔ cup (83 g) all-purpose flour*
¼ cup (50 g) light brown sugar
½ cup (118 ml) melted butter

* GLUTEN-FREE ALTERNATIVE
⅔ cup (105 g) brown rice flour

Preheat the oven to 400°F (204°C).

Lightly grease an 8-inch (20-cm) square pan or a 10-inch (25-cm) cast-iron skillet with butter. Rinse the berries and place them in a small bowl. Sprinkle with sugar, cornstarch, and cinnamon. Stir to coat.

In a separate bowl, combine the oats, coconut, flour, brown sugar, and butter. Stir with a fork to create a streusel-like topping. Scoop half the topping into the prepared pan. Lightly press to cover the bottom of the pan. Pour the berries over the crust, spreading them evenly across the pan. Sprinkle with the remaining crisp topping mixture.

Bake for 25 to 28 minutes, until golden brown. Let cool at least 10 minutes before scooping into bowls.

MAKE-AHEAD DIRECTIONS
Store this in an airtight container in the refrigerator for up to 3 days. Serve at room temperature or reheat in the microwave or covered in the oven.

Cook's Note: Frozen blueberries may be substituted for the fresh berries in this recipe. Blackberries and raspberries work well also. If you are using frozen berries, add 2 tablespoons (30 ml) of water and an additional 2 tablespoons (25 g) of sugar to the fruit mixture.

Sweet and Savory Snacks

These easy recipes are great for snacking throughout the day: morning, afternoon, or evening. Whether you're craving something salty in between breakfast and lunch, or need a sweet pick-me-up midafternoon, there's a snack here that's sure to satisfy that craving. It's so nice to have homemade snacks ready to pack and take along with you instead of picking up less-healthy foods when you're on the go.

A handful of Sweet and Spicy Roasted Mixed Nuts (page 164) is perfect for tucking into your bag when you're going to be out and about. Better-Than-Store-Bought Ranch Dip with Vegetables (page 167) is in our refrigerator 24/7. My kids grab the box of vegetables and the ranch dip out every afternoon to snack before dinner.

Coconut Oatmeal Trail Mix Cookies (page 163) are a chewy nut-and-coconut-filled cookie that will keep nicely for days. Peanut Butter Chocolate Chip Cookie Dough Bites (page 179) keep well in the refrigerator or the freezer. They're a fun, bite-size treat when you just want a little something sweet. If you have just ten minutes, you can whip up a batch of Perfect-Every-Time Brownies (page 180).

COCONUT OATMEAL TRAIL MIX COOKIES

<table>
<tr><td>Yield:
24 cookies</td><td>Chewy coconut-filled oatmeal cookies loaded with the best trail mix fillings are so easy to make the kids can pull them together in minutes. This is one of our favorite snack cookies, and they keep very nicely for several days in the pantry.

I like to make a double batch of the basic cookies and then split the dough up for different filling options. My favorite combination is pecans and raisins, but the chunky monkey cookies with banana chips and chocolate are a very close second.</td></tr>
</table>

½ cup (118 ml) melted butter

½ cup (160 g) light brown sugar

2 cups (312 g) old-fashioned rolled oats

2 eggs

1 cup (75 g) sweetened flaked coconut

FAVORITE ADD-IN COMBINATIONS

½ cup (55 g) chopped pecans or walnuts and ½ cup (60 g) raisins or dried cranberries

½ cup (114 g) roughly chopped or broken banana chips and ½ cup (84 g) semisweet chocolate chips

½ cup (84 g) white, dark, or semisweet chocolate chips and ½ cup (46 g) sliced almonds

⅔ cup (134 g) chopped dehydrated pineapple and ½ cup (55 g) chopped pecans

Preheat the oven to 325°F (163°C).

Stir the butter and brown sugar together until they're well combined. Add the oats and stir to mix. Add the eggs and coconut. Stir to combine. Add the additional ingredients of your choice, and stir once more.

Scoop 2-tablespoon (31-g) portions onto a parchment- or silicone-lined baking sheet. Lightly press the cookies and shape them with your hands, as needed. Bake for 15 minutes and then let cool for at least 5, preferably 10, minutes before removing to a wire rack or plate. Store in an airtight container.

Cook's Notes: Coconut oil may be substituted for the butter in this recipe.

This is a loose and crumbly cookie "dough." You'll need to press the cookies and shape them slightly with your hands after scooping them onto the cookie sheet.

SWEET AND SPICY ROASTED MIXED NUTS

Yield:
About
5 cups

Sweet and slightly spicy, these crunchy mixed nuts are a snack that my whole family loves. I like to pack a handful of these nuts in a bag for snacking in between meals on the busiest of days.

4 cups (548 g) mixed nuts

½ cup (100 g) light or dark brown sugar

½ to 1 tsp kosher salt

¼ tsp chili powder

¼ tsp paprika

½ tsp cayenne pepper

3 tbsp (45 ml) honey

2 tbsp (30 ml) water

2 tsp (10 ml) refined coconut oil or any unflavored oil

Preheat the oven to 350°F (177°C).

Place the nuts on a large baking sheet in a single layer. Toast in the oven until the nuts are fragrant, approximately 13 to 15 minutes. Watch them carefully; they will go from perfectly roasted to burned in just about a minute.

While the nuts are roasting, combine the sugar, salt, chili powder, paprika, and cayenne in a small bowl and set aside.

In a large cold saucepan, combine the honey, water, and oil. When the nuts come out of the oven, set them aside. Bring the saucepan to a boil and then reduce the heat to low. Add the nuts and cook, stirring every so often, until all the liquid has evaporated and the honey has thoroughly coated the nuts. This should take less than 5 minutes. The nuts will be shiny at this point.

Sprinkle the sugar mixture a few tablespoons at a time over the coated nuts. Stir well between each addition. Once all of the sugar is combined with the nuts, stir again to make sure everything is well coated. Spread the warm nuts in a single layer on top of parchment paper or a baking mat to cool. Use a couple of forks or your fingers to separate warm nuts if they clump together while they are cooling. Once cooled, store the nuts in an airtight container for up to 1 month.

Cook's Notes: Raw or roasted and salted nuts may be used to make this recipe. If you are using preroasted and salted nuts, use the lesser amount of salt in the recipe and skip the roasting step.

Any variety of nuts may be used to make this recipe. If almonds are your favorite, use only almonds. If pecans are the only nut your family will eat, it's fine to use only pecans.

BETTER-THAN-STORE-BOUGHT RANCH DIP WITH VEGETABLES

Yield:
About
2 cups
(227 g)

Tangy and filled with an abundance of dried herbs, this ranch dip tastes better than anything you can buy at the grocery store. I've been making homemade ranch dip for many years now. My boys stir together a batch of this dip each week as they prep our fresh vegetable box for snacking.

We keep a large box of fresh vegetables in the refrigerator ready for snacking through the week. I typically set it on the table as I'm making dinner. Sliced cucumbers, bell peppers, broccoli, carrots, and grape tomatoes are some of our favorite vegetables that we keep on hand for snacking.

1 cup (230 g) sour cream

½ cup (120 g) mayonnaise

1 tsp dried dill weed, adjust to taste

¾ tsp dried parsley

¾ tsp dried chives

½ tsp garlic powder

½ tsp onion powder

½ tsp fine sea salt

¼ tsp finely cracked pepper, adjust to taste

½ to 1 tbsp (8 to 15 ml) freshly squeezed lemon juice or plain white vinegar

FRESH VEGETABLES FOR DIPPING
Cucumbers

Carrots

Bell peppers

Broccoli

Grape tomatoes

Whisk together the sour cream, mayonnaise, dill, parsley, chives, garlic powder, onion powder, salt, pepper, and lemon juice. Cover and refrigerate until ready to serve. The flavors will increase after resting in the refrigerator. I like to make this a day in advance when possible. Serve with the veggies of your choice.

Cook's Note: Lemon juice is my first choice when making this dip. However, if I happen to be out of lemons, plain white vinegar works as well. We like a tangy ranch dip, so we use the full tablespoon (15 ml) of lemon juice or vinegar for this recipe. Feel free to adjust it for your tastes.

CINNAMON SOUR CREAM COFFEE CAKE

Yield:
8 to 12
servings

Cinnamon Sour Cream Coffee Cake layered with cinnamon streusel is a snack that I can't resist. Whether it's early in the morning with a cup of coffee, midafternoon, or late at night, this cake is a favorite. Heavy on the cinnamon streusel, this cake is literally half streusel. No one has been able to resist a slice yet.

CINNAMON STREUSEL LAYER
1⅓ cups (167 g) all-purpose flour*

¾ cup (150 g) brown sugar

1 tbsp (8 g) ground cinnamon

½ tsp ground nutmeg

¾ cup (177 ml) melted butter

* GLUTEN-FREE ALTERNATIVE
1⅓ cups (210 g) brown rice flour

CAKE INGREDIENTS
½ cup (114 g) butter, softened

1 cup (200 g) sugar

2 eggs

1 tsp vanilla extract

1 cup (125 g) all-purpose flour**

½ tsp baking powder

1 tsp ground cinnamon

½ cup (115 g) sour cream

** GLUTEN-FREE ALTERNATIVE
⅔ cup (105 g) brown rice flour

¼ cup (26 g) tapioca starch

¼ cup (44 g) potato starch

Preheat the oven to 350°F (177°C).

Grease a 10-inch (25-cm) square pan with butter. In a medium bowl, combine the flour, brown sugar, cinnamon, nutmeg, and butter. Stir with a fork until clumps form. Set aside.

In a large mixing bowl, beat the butter and the sugar together until light and fluffy, about 3 to 4 minutes. Stir in the eggs and vanilla extract. Add the flour, baking powder, and cinnamon. Stir to combine all the ingredients. Mix in the sour cream.

Pour half of the batter into the prepared pan. Use a spatula to spread a thin layer across the bottom of the pan. Sprinkle half the cinnamon streusel over the batter and spoon the remaining batter over the streusel layer. Sprinkle the remaining streusel over the batter in the pan.

Bake for 40 to 42 minutes, until lightly browned and a toothpick comes out with moist crumbs. Let cool completely before slicing.

Cook's Note: This cake freezes well. Wrap slices tightly in an airtight container or zip-top bags. Thaw at room temperature or reheat from frozen in the microwave.

CHEDDAR HAM CHEESEBALL WITH PECANS

Yield:
6 to 10 servings

This creamy cheeseball is filled with cheddar and ham. It's a fun snack that keeps nicely for several days. With some raw vegetables or crackers, this snack is a favorite with the whole family.

16 oz (454 g) cream cheese

½ lb (227 g) deli ham, roughly chopped

4 oz (113 g) cheddar, shredded

1 tbsp (16 g) Dijon mustard

1 tsp granulated garlic or garlic powder

½ tsp black pepper

¼ tsp kosher salt

1 cup (109 g) chopped pecans

FOR SERVING
Crackers

Pretzels

Tortilla chips

Vegetables

In a large mixing bowl, combine the cream cheese, ham, and cheddar cheese. Beat with an electric mixer until well combined. Add the mustard, garlic, pepper, and salt. Beat again to mix the seasonings thoroughly.

Place a sheet of plastic wrap on the counter. Scoop the cheeseball mixture onto the plastic wrap and roll into a ball. Refrigerate at least 1 hour.

Place the pecans in a pie plate or on a rimmed plate. Roll the chilled cheeseball in the pecans, pressing firmly to make them stick. Serve immediately or store in an airtight container and refrigerate until ready to serve. Serve with crackers, pretzels, tortilla chips, or vegetables for dipping.

Cook's Note: It works fine to skip the first refrigeration step; it just will be a little messier. Use a rubber spatula and your hands to form a ball when the ingredients have been combined. Roll the cheeseball in the pecans and then store as directed above.

CHOCOLATE CHIP TOFFEE BANANA BREAD

Yield:
2 loaves or
24 muffins

Rich chocolate-and-toffee-filled banana bread is a sweet treat that comes together in very little time. This bread freezes beautifully and reheats in seconds. I love this bread with a hot cup of coffee, and my boys love it for an afternoon snack with a glass of milk.

½ cup (114 g) butter, softened

1 cup (200 g) light brown sugar

1 tsp vanilla extract

2 eggs

1½ cups (188 g) all-purpose flour*

1 tsp baking soda

1 tsp kosher salt

½ tsp ground cinnamon

¼ tsp ground nutmeg

4 medium bananas, very ripe, about 1½ cups (338 g) mashed

½ cup (115 g) sour cream

1 cup (168 g) chocolate chips, divided

¾ cup (180 g) toffee chips, divided

* GLUTEN-FREE ALTERNATIVE
1¼ cups (198 g) brown rice flour

⅓ cup (35 g) tapioca starch

¼ cup (44 g) potato starch

Preheat the oven to 350°F (177°C).

Grease two 8½ × 4½-inch (21.5 × 10-cm) loaf pans very thoroughly, or line with parchment. Alternatively, line 24 muffin cups with paper liners and spray the liners very lightly with nonstick spray.

In a mixing bowl, combine the butter and sugar, and beat with a mixer until smooth. Add the vanilla and eggs, and beat until smooth. In a separate bowl, whisk together the flour, baking soda, salt, cinnamon, and nutmeg. Slowly add the dry ingredients to the wet ingredients, beating just until they're combined.

Add the bananas and sour cream, and stir just until they're combined. Stir in ¾ cup (126 g) of chocolate chips and ½ cup (120 g) of toffee chips. Pour the mixture into the prepared pans or muffin tins. Sprinkle with the reserved chocolate chips and toffee chips. Bake the full-size loaf pans for 55 to 60 minutes and the muffins for 20 to 22 minutes, until an inserted toothpick comes out with moist crumbs. Let the loaves cool completely before sliding a knife around the edge of the pan to loosen and then remove to a plate or wire rack.

Cook's Note: This bread will keep nicely in the freezer for 2 to 3 months. If you're freezing the muffins, simply cool and store in a zip-top bag. To freeze the loaf, I recommend cooling completely and then wrapping the unsliced loaf in foil before placing in a large zip-top bag.

SWEET AND SALTY PRETZEL NUT CEREAL BARS

Yield:
12 servings

Crunchy, chewy, gooey, nutty, sweet, and salty snack bars are a guaranteed win with everyone. These bars will keep nicely for several days, making them perfect for packing into lunches or grabbing between school, work, and soccer practice.

6 tbsp (90 g) butter

8 cups (400 g) miniature marshmallows, divided

5½ cups (568 g) crisp rice cereal

2 cups (464 g) pretzel twists

1 cup (144 g) roasted salted peanuts

STOVE TOP DIRECTIONS

Melt the butter in a large pot over medium heat. Add 6 cups (300 g) of marshmallows and stir until they begin to melt and stick together. Remove from the heat.

Add the cereal to the pot and stir until well coated. Add the pretzels, peanuts, and additional marshmallows, and stir to combine.

Scoop the sticky cereal mixture onto a parchment-lined baking sheet or 9 × 13-inch (23 × 33-cm) pan. Use a lightly buttered spatula or your slightly wet hands to gently press the mixture across the pan, being careful not to press too firmly. Let cool for a few minutes before slicing. Store in an airtight container.

MICROWAVE DIRECTIONS

Combine the butter and 6 cups (300 g) of marshmallows in a large glass mixing bowl and microwave for 2 minutes at full power. Remove from the microwave and stir until the marshmallows begin to melt and stick together. (If the marshmallows haven't yet melted, microwave up to an additional 30 seconds, only as needed.)

Add the cereal to the bowl and stir until well coated. Add the pretzels, peanuts, and additional marshmallows, and stir to combine. Scoop the sticky cereal mixture onto a parchment-lined baking sheet or 9 × 13-inch (23 × 33-cm) pan. Use a lightly buttered spatula or your slightly wet hands to gently press the mixture across the pan, being careful not to press too firmly. Let cool for a few minutes before slicing. Store in an airtight container.

Cook's Note: The humidity where you live will affect how long these bars will keep. They last several days in my climate before they are too crunchy to enjoy. In a more humid environment, they will grow softer with time.

PINEAPPLE JALAPEÑO SALSA

Yield:
About 2 cups
(520 g)

Sweet bits of pineapple and spicy jalapeño combine to make this salsa one of our favorite snacks. If this salsa is in the refrigerator, it's impossible for any of us to resist it. It's great with a bowl of chips, on a burger, or with chicken or fish.

1 small pineapple, peeled, cored, and very finely diced, about 2½ cups (413 g)

1 large jalapeño, seeded and finely minced, about 2 tbsp (28 g), add more for a spicier bite

1 tbsp (15 ml) fresh lime juice, about 1 small lime

¼ cup (4 g) fresh cilantro (leaves only), finely chopped

3 green onions, very thinly sliced, about 2 tbsp (5 g)

¼ tsp kosher salt, adjust to taste

⅛ tsp freshly ground black pepper, adjust to taste

Place the pineapple, jalapeño, lime juice, cilantro, green onions, salt, and pepper in a bowl, and stir to combine. Cover with a lid or transfer to an airtight container. Chill until ready to serve. This will keep well in the refrigerator for about a week.

PEANUT BUTTER CHOCOLATE CHIP COOKIE DOUGH BITES

Yield:
2 dozen cookie dough bites

If your weakness for cookie dough is even greater than your love for fresh cookies, this is the snack for you. These sweet chocolate peanut butter bites are a great afternoon pick-me-up, and I love to grab a couple from the freezer to help me power through the end of my day's work.

These cookie dough bites taste just like cookie dough and will keep in the refrigerator for up to 3 days or in the freezer for 2 months. (Not that mine have ever lasted that long!)

½ cup (114 g) butter, room temperature

½ cup (129 g) peanut butter

½ cup (100 g) light brown sugar

2 tsp (10 ml) vanilla extract

¼ tsp baking soda

1½ cups (188 g) all-purpose flour*

¾ cup (60 g) quick oats

2 tbsp (30 ml) milk, as needed

¾ to 1 cup (130 to 173 g) mini chocolate chips

* GLUTEN-FREE ALTERNATIVE
Add an additional 1½ cups (234 g) quick oats and omit the all-purpose flour.

In a bowl, place the butter, peanut butter, brown sugar, and vanilla, and beat until smooth and creamy. Add the baking soda, flour, and oats. Stir to combine. If the mixture is too dry to roll into balls, add the milk. Stir in the chocolate chips. Scoop out the dough and roll into 1-inch (2.5-cm) balls. Store in the refrigerator until ready to eat.

Cook's Notes: Old-fashioned oats may be substituted for the quick oats in this recipe. The texture is a little more defined with the larger oats.

There is a bit of a debate over eating raw flour, so if that bothers you, follow the gluten-free directions.

PERFECT-EVERY-TIME BROWNIES

Yield:
12 to 16 brownies

Who doesn't love a rich, fudgy brownie for a sweet snack? Whether you're looking for an over-the-top chocolate indulgence or a salty-sweet, nut-filled treat, one of these brownies is sure to satisfy your sweet tooth. This is a simple saucepan recipe that comes together in about 10 minutes, making it perfect for snacking any time of day.

½ cup (114 g) butter

2 cups (336 g) semisweet chocolate chips

1 cup (200 g) light brown sugar

1 tbsp (15 ml) vanilla extract

4 eggs

1 cup (125 g) all-purpose flour*

½ tsp kosher salt

* GLUTEN-FREE ALTERNATIVE
⅔ cup (105 g) brown rice flour
⅓ cup (35 g) tapioca starch

ADD-IN OPTIONS
1 cup (109 g) chopped pecans and ½ cup (84 g) semisweet chocolate chips

¾ cup (70 g) sweetened shredded coconut and 12 caramels, cut into 4 pieces each, scattered on top of the brownies

½ cup (84 g) white chocolate chips and ½ cup (84 g) dark chocolate chips

1 cup (134 g) chopped mixed nuts: peanuts, macadamia, pecans, walnuts, or almonds

½ cup (120 ml) caramel sauce, swirled into brownies, and ¼ cup (84 g) semisweet chocolate, sprinkled on top

Preheat the oven to 325°F (163°C).

Melt the butter in a medium saucepan over medium-high heat. Add the chocolate chips and stir until they're melted. Remove the pan from the heat. Add the brown sugar and vanilla, and stir until smooth.

Whisk in the eggs. Add the flour and salt. Stir until well combined. Stir in your choice of add-ins. Pour into a well-greased or parchment-lined 9 × 13-inch (23 × 33-cm) pan. Bake for 30 to 34 minutes, until a toothpick inserted in the center of the brownies comes out with moist crumbs.

Cook's Notes: These brownies will keep nicely in an airtight container at room temperature for several days. Alternatively, they can be wrapped airtight and frozen for up to 3 months. Thaw at room temperature before eating.

To make 2 different kinds of brownies, divide the batter between 2 8-inch (20-cm) square pans, and split the suggested amounts for topping combinations in half to make 2 different recipes at once. Baking time for 2 8-inch (20-cm) square pans is 28 to 30 minutes.

Seasoning Mixes

Cajun, Italian, and Mexican seasoning mixes, along with my beloved Crazy Salt, have had dedicated spaces in my spice cabinet for years now. The beauty of a seasoning blend is most clear on the days when I'm rushed in the kitchen. It makes a big difference just to sprinkle the seasoning mix versus pulling out half a dozen or more different spices.

I'm never willing to skimp on flavor in my hurry to get a meal on the table, so these spice blends cut the cooking time down and keep things flavorful. Feel free to multiply the seasoning mixes however you like. I typically double or triple these recipes and keep them ready to use in my spice cabinet.

CAJUN SEASONING MIX

Yield: About ¼ cup (35 g)	This Cajun spice blend is the first thing I reach for anytime I'm cooking with potatoes. I love the flavor it adds to any recipe, though, and you'll see it used throughout this book.

1 tbsp (7 g) smoked paprika or plain paprika

1 tbsp (3 g) granulated garlic or garlic powder

2 tsp (12 g) kosher salt

2 tsp (4 g) freshly ground black pepper

2 tsp (2 g) granulated onion or onion powder

2 tsp (2 g) crushed oregano

2 tsp (2 g) crushed thyme

1 tsp cayenne pepper

Place all the herbs and spices in a small jar. Seal with a lid and shake to combine. Store the spices in an airtight container until you're ready to use them.

CRAZY SALT SEASONING MIX

Yield: About ½ cup (84 g)	I use Crazy Salt Seasoning Mix on eggs, meat, popcorn, vegetables, French fries, and any kind of potato. You can use this spice blend anywhere you might want a sprinkling of salt, but it is especially amazing on eggs. Eggs just aren't eggs in my house without the Crazy Salt.

¼ cup (72 g) kosher salt

4 tsp (11 g) granulated garlic

1 tbsp (7 g) freshly ground black pepper

2 tsp (2 g) granulated onion

½ tsp celery salt

½ tsp cayenne pepper

¼ tsp finely crushed sage (optional)

Place all the herbs and spices in a small jar. Seal with a lid and shake to combine. Store the spices in an airtight container until you're ready to use them.

Cook's Note: You can pulse all the spices in a blender for a finer, more uniform consistency or simply stir them together in a jar. I tend to measure Crazy Salt Seasoning Mix in finger pinches, the same way I use kosher salt, so the jar method works great for me. Just shake the jar if the spices begin to separate.

ITALIAN SEASONING MIX

Yield: About ¼ cup (18 g)	Italian Seasoning Mix combines classic Italian flavors in an easy-to-use dried blend of herbs. Not only is this my favorite soup seasoning, but I also use this blend of herbs for pasta sauces, potatoes, and roasted meats.

1 tbsp (3 g) dried basil

1 tbsp (3 g) dried oregano

1 tbsp (3 g) dried thyme

1 tbsp (3 g) dried marjoram

2 tsp (2 g) dried sage

1 tbsp (3 g) dried rosemary

Place the basil, oregano, thyme, marjoram, and sage in a small jar. Lightly crush the large pieces of rosemary with your fingers before adding it to the jar. Seal the jar with a lid and shake to combine. Store the herbs in an airtight container until you're ready to use them.

MEXICAN SEASONING MIX

Yield: About 1 cup (135 g)	This blend of Mexican herbs and spices has lived in my kitchen for years now. The seasoning mix can be used in any recipe that calls for taco seasoning. The beauty of this recipe is the ability to adjust the heat however you like it best. If you find it a bit spicy, reduce the chili powder and pepper. Want a little more kick? Increase them.

½ cup (56 g) chili powder

4 tbsp (28 g) ground cumin

2 tbsp (34 g) kosher salt

2 tbsp (13 g) black pepper

4 tsp (9 g) smoked paprika

2 tsp (2 g) crushed red pepper flakes

2 tsp (2 g) dried oregano

2 tsp (2 g) granulated garlic or garlic powder

2 tsp (2 g) granulated onion or onion powder

1 tsp (2 g) cayenne pepper (optional)

Place all the herbs and spices in a small jar. Seal with a lid and shake to combine. Store the spices in an airtight container until you're ready to use them.

Cook's Note: If you have access to it, New Mexico chili powder is my choice for this spice mixture and for any other recipe that calls for chili powder. You should be able to find it in spice pouches in the Mexican food section of most grocery stores.

Acknowledgments

Sean: You have never failed to believe in me. Thanks for supporting me through everything and encouraging me to reach for my dreams. This life with you is an amazing ride, and I wouldn't trade it for anything.

Sam: From the never-ending jokes so bad that they're funny to the late-night conversations that make me laugh and sigh, it's pure joy to watch you as a teenager. Thank you for doing the 72,943 dishes that made this book possible.

Ben: You are my sunshine, my thunderstorm, my child for whom I dream of endless possibilities. Watching you learn to cook on your own over the past year has been a whole lot of fun. I am overwhelmingly proud of you.

Nate: Thank you for helping me cook, dreaming up recipes, and never failing to give an honest opinion on it all. You make my heart so happy.

Mom: Thank you more than you will ever know for all of your help with the kids this year. There's nothing better than knowing our boys love hanging out with the best grandma in the world.

Jenny: You are my forever cheerleader. Your phone calls are priceless moments in my mornings.

Heather and Karl: Your enthusiasm and willingness to taste all of the recipes were a joy to watch. I promise there won't be an egg-filled breakfast every day of your visit next year.

Sandra: Thank you for helping me endlessly over the past few years. This job wouldn't be nearly as fun without you.

Christi, Holly, Lynne, Meseidy, and Rebecca: You girls are my dolls forever and amen. There is no one else with whom I'd rather laugh, shoot video, eat too much food, shoot video, laugh, shoot video, and laugh again.

To my fellow bloggers: You inspire me every single day. This job that we are lucky enough to do, it's pretty amazing.

To every person who tested a recipe: Whether you cooked, baked, or simply tasted a recipe, you have helped make this cookbook all that it is.

To my readers: I am blessed every day to call you my friends. My life is a better place for having you in my corner of the Internet.

Sarah, Will, and the whole team at Page Street: Thank you for everything.

"Trust in the Lord with all your heart, and lean not on your own understanding; in all your ways acknowledge Him, and He shall direct your paths." (Proverbs 3:5–6, New King James Version)

About the Author

Mary Younkin, creator of the recipe website Barefeet in the Kitchen and author of *The Weeknight Dinner Cookbook*, brings her love for family meals to her second cookbook, *The Weekday Lunches & Breakfasts Cookbook*.

She wasn't always a great cook, but she applied her keen organization and study skills to the task and became a fantastic force in the kitchen. Her loyal readers, family, and friends have come to rely on her solidly tested, excellent, family-friendly recipes.

Her new book makes homemade lunches and breakfasts every day of the week not only achievable, but easy and enjoyable as well.

Mary lives in the Phoenix area of Arizona with her husband, children, and an extensive collection of spatulas and whisks.

Index